THE SOCIETY

of

ST. VINCENT DE PAUL

PHOENIX

Frank M. Barrios

THE
History
PRESS

Published by The History Press
Charleston, SC
www.historypress.com

First published 2020
Manufactured in the United States

ISBN 9781467144681

Library of Congress Control Number: 2020941939

CONTENTS

ACKNOWLEDGEMENTS

The Society of St. Vincent de Paul (SVdP) is a unique charitable organization that has very few limits to what it will do to help those who are in need of assistance: "No work of charity is foreign to the society." It should be emphasized, however, that there are very strict rules as to how that assistance can be administered while remaining open to all forms of charitable assistance.

When SVdP began in Phoenix, Arizona, it consisted of only a few members; everyone knew what others were accomplishing. But as the organization grew, providing assistance to several counties in Arizona, it became more difficult for any one person to know all that was occurring. As a consequence, many people were consulted in order to define the history of SVdP Phoenix. To list all the people who provided historical information would require an unimaginably long list of individuals. Although they are not listed in this book, their contributions are important and appreciated. There were a few individuals, however, who were indispensable to the writing of this book. I owe sincere gratitude to Jessica Berg, Alejandra Bucon, Jerry Castro, Erica Hodges, Steve Jenkins, Susan Junker, Charlotte and Joe Riley, David Smith and Gary Weian. I would like to say a special thank-you to Steve Zabilski, the current executive director, and Gary Brown, a past executive director.

It would not be right to only acknowledge those who are leaders and managers and not give credit to the volunteers and members who are the core of the society's success—the frontline soldiers in the war against poverty. There were many individuals who dedicated major parts of their lives to SVdP. There were also many members of religious orders who saw the success of the society's mission to help the poor and joined in the effort. Both priests and nuns provided assistance, from bishops to retired priests and nuns from various orders. Countless volunteers and SVdP Phoenix members who were not part of the paid staff engaged in this work, people who believed in SVdP's mission and dedicated large portions of their lives to assisting the poor. It would be impossible to list them all. Andy Andreano and Duane Tegler, though they have passed on, were two individuals, in particular, who will not be forgotten for their contributions to SVdP's mission here in Phoenix.

Unless otherwise noted, all images are courtesy of the Diocesan Council for the Society of St. Vincent de Paul, Diocese of Phoenix (SVdP Phoenix).

SOCIETY OF ST. VINCENT DE PAUL
DIOCESE OF PHOENIX
MISSION STATEMENT

The mission of the Society of St. Vincent de Paul Diocese of Phoenix is to offer person-to-person service to the needy and suffering, regardless of race, origin, religion or gender. Inspired by Gospel values, the society encourages the spiritual growth of its members, volunteers, the people they serve and benefactors; it encourages fellowship while serving those in need; and provides an opportunity for others to serve those in need.

➤ Spirituality

➤ Fellowship

➤ Serving Those in Need

➤ Giving Others the Opportunity to Serve

INTRODUCTION

Today, the Society of St. Vincent de Paul (SVdP) is found in more than 150 countries around the world and has a presence in about 4,500 locations throughout the United States. To the surprise of many, the Diocesan Council for the Society of St. Vincent de Paul, Diocese of Phoenix (SVdP Phoenix) is the largest council in the world. Since the whispers of the establishment of SVdP Phoenix only began in St. Mary's Church in 1946, the question arises of what has made it so successful so quickly. This book will document the story of that success and how the society followed in the footsteps of Frederic Ozanam and St. Vincent de Paul.

When we speak of the success of SVdP Phoenix, we must acknowledge that leadership has played a major role in its development. The society has been blessed with great leaders who have dedicated themselves to assisting those living in poverty. We have been blessed with spiritual and capable leadership by our presidents and board members, but in particular, the society has received a special blessing with the selection of executive directors who have provided the daily leadership that was needed to bring the society to where it is today.

Steve Zabilski currently serves as the executive director and has done so for more than twenty-three years. Zabilski's skills, combined with his dedication, have brought SVdP Phoenix through both good and difficult times and have directed the organization to the prosperous times of today. His name is synonymous with SVdP around the valley, and the relationship he has developed with the local community provides one of the greatest

Left: Stephen J. Zabilski, executive director, Phoenix Diocesan Council of St. Vincent de Paul (SVdP Phoenix) (1996 to present).

Right: Shannon Clancy, associate executive director and chief philanthropy officer, Phoenix Diocesan Council of St. Vincent de Paul (2002 to present).

assets of the organization. Previous executive directors Gary Brown, Bob Bosler and Chris Becker all helped to construct the solid foundation that Zabilski inherited and allowed him to build on the successes of the past.

We specially acknowledge Shannon Clancy for all the work she has accomplished as the associate executive director of SVdP Phoenix. Clancy continues to work closely with Zabilski and all our members and staff to help make our organization one of the best in the world.

SVdP is a Catholic lay organization and operates independently from the Catholic diocesan form of government. Even so, the society is Catholic and obedient to Catholic teachings. As such, conferences are normally established within the boundaries of the Catholic parishes of the controlling diocese. With permission from the parish pastor, the society agrees to serve the poor within the parish boundaries; in return, the pastor provides operating space within the parish. In 2019, with permission from the pastors of the Phoenix Diocese Catholic Churches, SVdP Phoenix was located in eighty-one of the ninety-four Catholic parishes within the diocese. The society has been blessed by the support received from the Catholic Diocese of Phoenix. It especially thanks current bishops Olmsted and Nevares for the boundless support they continue to provide.

Some important parts of the society's ministry are the services it provides through the Catholic parishes (conferences) of the Phoenix Diocese. SVdP

Bishop Thomas J. Olmsted, Bishop, Catholic Diocese of Phoenix, helping out at the SVdP Phoenix Dan O'Meara Center.

Bob Hernandez, member of the St. Matthews conference, Phoenix, preparing for a home visit.

Phoenix is a face-to-face ministry; when assistance is requested at the parish level, the society responds by visiting homes and directly providing assistance. Most requests are for food, but when conference financial resources allow, rent and utility assistance may be provided. All home visits are made by at least two people; if the clients agree, the visit is concluded with a joint prayer.

As will be shown in this book, SVdP Phoenix also has a large presence separate from the parish boundaries. In 2019, the society's annual operating budget was $35 million, and its membership comprised 3,500 individuals. Approximately 225 full-time paid staff see to the day-to-day operations of the organization. This dedicated, well-disciplined staff shares with Vincentian members a commitment to serve those in need. In fact, many paid employees regularly donate funds to support the mission. The organization has always paid fair wages to its employees and strives to exceed the minimum wage whenever possible.

The staff's role is to implement the services provided by SVdP Phoenix. One of the ways staff interacts with Vincentian volunteers is through the committee process. In 2019, there were ten working committees that defined existing policy and recommend changes if necessary, submitting their findings to the board of directors or the general membership for approval. Certainly, this excellent working relationship contributes to the society's great success in serving the community.

SVdP Phoenix is a well-known charity within the Phoenix Diocese. Its open policy allows it to directly reach those in need. We remain transparent in all of our activities and are blessed with ongoing support from public media, including newspapers and radio and television stations. A monthly electronic newsletter is distributed by email to approximately three thousand Vincentians. The society's larger, more professional newsletter, the *Vincentian Connection*, with a circulation of seventy-eight thousand, is mailed twice a year. This successful outreach is both noticed and appreciated throughout the community. Individuals and organizations see the society's effectiveness and correspondingly help support its efforts to continue its work. Excellent fiscal management, a detailed budget process and utilizing large numbers of volunteers keep overhead low, maximizing the funds available to serve the community.

Community assistance is essential to the services that the society provides, and it thanks and prays for all those individuals and organizations that support it. This assistance allows the society to feed the hungry through its kitchen and dining rooms, and yes, it even grows its own food in its three urban farms. Clothing and furniture are provided through the society's thrift stores, and transitional housing is provided at Ozanam Manor and through the Resource Center. Health and dental care are available at the society's medical and dental clinics and the family wellness center. St. Anne's Ministry loans medical equipment. Programs for children, teens and young adults are offered in the Dream Center and through the society's One at a Time scholarship program.

It is important to emphasize that SVdP Phoenix serves all who are in need, without qualification except need. This means that the society serves anyone without regard to race, origin, religion, legal status or gender. SVdP Phoenix strongly promotes understanding, cooperation and mutual love among people of different cultures, religions, ethnic backgrounds and social groups, and so, it contributes to the peace and unity of all people.

SVDP CHRONOLOGY 1946-2020

Matt Scott, president, 1949–65.

1946: St. Mary's Conference formed by five men.

1949: Three conferences joined to form Particular Council.

1950: First thrift store opened.

1952: First charity dining room opened.

1954: Dining room moved to Ninth Avenue and Madison Street

Dan O'Meara, president, 1965–68.

1965: SVdP grows to twenty-five parish conferences.

Joe Connors, president, 1968–74.

1969: Diocese of Phoenix formed.

Women are officially invited to join the society.

Mort Staub, president, 1974–80.

1977: Free medical and dental clinic opened.

1978: New warehouse built.

Jim Finnerty, president, 1980–86.

1981: Transient aid center opened.

1982: Operation of temporary homeless shelter began.

1984: Society served 10 millionth meal.

Society began its Ministry to the Homeless.

1985: Ozanam Manor, a transitional shelter, founded.

Ministry to the Incarcerated created.

Ron Meyer, president, 1986–89.

1987: Watkins Road complex built.

1988: Sister conference in Cuernavaca, Mexico, formed.

Jim Finnerty, president, 1989–90.

1990: Mesa Dining Room purchased.

Terry Wilson, president, 1990–96.

1991: Society served 15 millionth meal.

Central kitchen and dining room opened on Watkins Road.

1994: New medical and dental clinic opened on Watkins Road.

1996: Conferences increased to seventy-eight.

New dining room in Sunnyslope opened.

 Nancy Spencer, president, 1996–2002.

1997: Medical equipment loans begun.

1998: "Need a Hand" cards introduced.

2000: Began "Hearts and Hands" family volunteer days.

2001: Sunnyslope thrift store opened.

Voice of the Poor advocacy committee formed in Phoenix.

One at a Time scholarship program established.

 Steve Jenkins, president, 2002–08.

2004: Society served 30 millionth meal.

2005: New Henry Unger Dining Room opened on the new human services campus.

Hurricane Katrina evacuees in Phoenix receive help from SVdP.

Terry Wilson appointed national vice president.

2006: Began serving breakfast at the Henry Unger Dining Room.

Joe Riley, president, 2008–14.

Frank Barrios, president, 2014–17.

Steve Attwood, president, 2017–Present.

2018: A brand-new building housing Ozanam Manor and the resource center opened.

1

WHO AND WHAT IS THE SOCIETY OF ST. VINCENT DE PAUL?

1833 to 1946

Every religion in the world identifies with helping the poor and those in need. Christianity is based on the belief in Jesus Christ and in the biblical doctrine of His life. In the Christian Bible, Christ is quoted as saying, "Whatsoever you do for the least of my brethren, you do for me" (Matthew 25:30). In other words, when Christians help those who are poor and in need of assistance, they are providing assistance directly to Jesus Christ. Taking Him at His word, many of His followers have long practiced charity in His name. As examples, the Middle Ages were marked by the building of hospitals and the founding of charities to serve the poor. In the High Middle Ages, the Franciscans arose as a religious order, and they were especially devoted to the poor and embracing a life of poverty. Later, the victims of the Black Death were largely tended to by those who believed in Jesus's words. The nineteenth century's whole idea of establishing medical missions abroad came from the same source. All of these efforts harked back to the idea of loving one's neighbor as oneself.

Yet, throughout the Christian world, history has found a world full of indifference, rationalizations and outright evil. On top of that, all efforts to spread the Word were limited by the technologies of the day to (greater or lesser) localities, where heroic individuals continued to fight for justice and charity. By the time of the Renaissance, the Christian world was often dominated by nobility and royalty who saw its members as literally a different breed from the common man. Their blood was "blue blood," and they married only among their own. Even the upper clergy were the province

St. Vincent de Paul.

of the nobility, and most of them cared primarily about money and politics. Even gross abuses like slavery and serfdom were not finally abandoned until the middle of the nineteenth century, often with struggle and bloodshed.

Yet, the idea of universal charity as a duty laid on man by God lived on. In 1581, a man was born in Pouy, France, whose legacy for charity became the inspiration for the identity of the Society of St. Vincent de Paul. St. Vincent de Paul is now the patron saint of those in need, but he was not born a saint. He was the third child of a fairly prosperous peasant farmer. There seemed nothing remarkable about him. An ambitious, practical and intelligent child, he showed no signs of wanting anything more than a comfortable life. A local lawyer helped him attend school, and eventually, he became a priest. At that time, this was often only a sign that a man wanted to rise in station; Vincent, after all, was a peasant, a member of the great third estate that made up 90 percent of the population of France. People like him were to pray, pay (most of the taxes) and obey. There is no sign that he considered this in any way unusual. He was certainly not a revolutionary.

Shortly after his ordination, Father Vincent was captured at sea by Muslim slavers and taken to Tunis in North Africa, where he was sold into slavery. He went from master to master, sometimes learning medicine, sometimes farming, until he escaped by sea and returned to Europe. This experience, though dire, did not seem to essentially change him. A papal legate discovered him and took him to Rome, where his winning personality brought him to the attention of the ruling classes. His agreeable personality helped him become a chaplain to the queen of France, who, as she aged, gained a genuine devotion to the poor, demanding that her chaplains visit them.

This led to the great crisis of Father Vincent's life, an internal war between his desire for prosperity and his own growing devotion to the poor, for he genuinely loved helping them and increasingly found his spiritual life quickened by serving them. After some harsh but effective spiritual direction, he finally realized that he would never find inner peace unless he dedicated

St. Louise de Marillac.

himself to the service of God through helping the poor. He accepted his first parish and found himself happy. But then, he was recalled to the ministry of a noble family and the people living on their estates. This quickly led to a spiritual revival among the peasantry and Father Vincent's founding of the Congregation of the Mission, a group of priests dedicated to founding missions among the country peasants. The group was duly formed in 1625.

Father Vincent then met one of the greatest influences in his life, Sister Louise de Marillac. Before her husband died, Sister Louise had a vision that, someday, she would meet a spiritual director; in the vision, she saw his face. After her husband's death, Sister Louise met Father Vincent de Paul and recognized him as the promised director. For several years, they corresponded, with Father Vincent stressing the need for inner peace. Sister Louise worked with Confraternities of Charity, and eventually, she convinced Father Vincent of the value of recruiting her into the leadership of the Company of the Daughters of Charity of St. Vincent de Paul. There, she became invaluable in overcoming the differences between the social classes of the poor and the bourgeoisie and aristocracy who wanted to help them. She recruited the young and humble. "Love the poor and honor them as you would Christ himself," she said. The Daughters of Charity were officially recognized in 1655.

When Father Vincent died in 1660, he had a substantial number of followers, including the Daughters of Charity, who were spread over several nations and colonies. The days were approaching when the organization might straddle the globe. Sister Louise died only months later.

In the following two centuries, France underwent the Revolution of 1789, a half dozen monarchies, two empires, two republics and innumerable coups, wars and insurrections. Yet, the poor were just as badly off as though the *Rights of Man* had never been announced by Thomas Paine. But the ideal of universal human charity did not die, even though the upper classes' tolerance of poverty continued. In 1831, when France had just overthrown the last of the Bourbon kings, in one of the country's tottering steps towards democracy, a new king, Louis Phillipe, was elected.

It was at this time that Frederic Ozanam, the founder of St. Vincent de Paul, was born.

Ozanam was a brilliant man of poetic and scholarly disposition who developed an early passion for the restoration of Catholicism in a secularized world that had remained just as corrupt as it had been during the time of St. Vincent de Paul. Rationalism, which was strongly opposed to Catholicism, had taken over the University of Paris, and Ozanam, along with seven followers, undertook the role of defending Christianity. In one debate, he was challenged to prove the truth of Christianity through works, not words. He took the attack seriously. He asked his followers if, in the course of one year's effort, they had made a single convert for Jesus Christ. They had not. "Yes," said Ozanam, "there is one thing wanting…works of charity! The blessing of the poor is the blessing of God." His challenger answered, "What are you doing for the poor? Where are the tangible results which will alone teach us the practical value of your faith? We await them, for it is only through them that we shall be converted." That very night, Ozanam ransacked his apartment for fuel and took it to an old, poor widow's apartment. He told his handful of followers, "We must do what is most agreeable to God. Therefore, we must do what our Lord Jesus Christ did when preaching the Gospel. Let us go to the poor." Paul Lamanche, an early companion, remembered, "I can still see the flame burning in Ozanam's eyes. I can hear his voice trembling a little with emotion as he explained…his project of a charitable Catholic association."

Ozanam founded the Council of Charity, with St. Vincent de Paul as its patron saint (this became the Society of St. Vincent de Paul). The group's goal was to create a lay organization that would at once help the poor and aid its members' spiritual growth. This goal expressed itself in an absolute loathing of gathering attention to one's good works. Ozanam said, "Without meekness, zeal for the salvation of souls is like a ship without sails."

In 1833, Ozanam and his followers began seeking advice from Sister Rosalie Rendu, now Blessed Rosalie Rendu, a daughter of charity who had become the human center for aid to the poor in France and the leading member of the Sisters of Charity in Paris. She opened a free clinic, a pharmacy, a school, a childcare center and a home for the elderly. "One of the greatest ways to help the poor is to show them respect and consideration," she said. Like Ozanam, she bridged the gap between the poor and those who wanted to be their benefactors, but she did not know how to go about getting around the barriers created by social class. It was very easy for the privileged who wanted to help the poor and had the means to do so to appear

Left: Blessed Frederic Ozanam. *Right*: Blessed Rosalie Rendu.

condescending, especially when their assistance seemed only a product of good manners. "The poor will insult you," Blessed Rosalie Rendu said. "The ruder they are, the more dignified you must be. Remember, our Lord hides behind those rags."

Ozanam expressed his love for the poor by likening them to Christ, only they were visible. "We see them with human eyes; they are there, and we can put our fingers and our hand in their wounds…and we should fall at their feet and say to them with the apostle…you are my Lord and my God." His attitude toward money and need became common throughout SVdP. "I am very much persuaded," he said, "that in the case of charity works, one must never worry about pecuniary resources—some always come along." Allied to this was his strong belief in the necessity of expansion for growth. He also strongly believed in what he called Christian Democracy, another abiding feature in Vincentian life. This attitude also served latter-day Vincentians in twentieth-century Phoenix.

Armed with the names of the poor Rendu provided them, the young Vincentians began going two by two into the slums, armed with baskets of food and coal to visit "the poorest of the poor." They always believed in justice as well as charity. The money they received from good parishioners was not to be used for the lazy or those who could help themselves. Assured on his deathbed in 1853 that he would have a heavenly reward for all his work, Ozanam is said to have replied, "I have already seen the glory of God in the faces of the poor."

Blessed Rosalie Rendu died soon after Ozanam, in 1856, but by that time, SVdP had come to the United States. The first American conference was formed in St. Louis, Missouri, in 1845. The associate pastor of the Cathedral of St. Louis, Father Ambrose Heim, helped establish the Society with twenty people, and he became its first spiritual advisor. Father Heim understood from the beginning that SVdP was a lay organization that had to be led by the laity. The idea quickly took hold, and by 1856, the organization had spread to New York City, Buffalo and Milwaukee. The SVdP in the United States was divided into eight regions. The East Region's first conference was established in Philadelphia in 1851; the Mid-East was established in Louisville in 1855; the Mid-West was established in St. Louis in 1845; the North-Central was established in Milwaukee in 1849; the Northeast was established in New York in 1847; the South-Central was established in San Antonio in 1871; the Southeast was established in New Orleans in 1858; and the West was established in San Francisco in 1860. In 2020, St. Vincent de Paul in the United States will celebrate its 175-year anniversary. A special event was held on Sunday, January 26, 2020, in Washington, D.C. mass was celebrated at the Basilica of the National Shrine of the Immaculate Conception, followed by the dedication and later installation of a mosaic of Blessed Frederic Ozanam in the Vincentian Chapel.

SVdP continued to grow from its humble beginning in 1845 into an organization of one hundred thousand members in 2020, when this book was completed.

The first five rules of the Society of St. Vincent de Paul are:

1. To follow Christ through service to those in need and so to bear witness to His compassionate and liberating love. Members show their commitment through person-to-person contact.
2. No work of charity is foreign to the society. It includes any form of help that alleviates suffering or deprivation and promotes human dignity and personal integrity in all their dimensions.
3. The society serves those in need, regardless of creed, ethnic or social background, health, gender or political opinions.
4. Vincentians strive to seek out and find those in need and the forgotten, the victims of exclusion or adversity.

5. Faithful to the spirit of its founders, the society constantly strives for renewal, adapting to changing world conditions. It seeks to be ever aware of the changes that occur in human society and the new types of poverty that may be identified or anticipated. It gives priority to the poorest of the poor and to those who are most rejected by society.

There are dozens more rules, including the very practical ones that say conferences must meet at least once every two weeks and that Vincentians must always make sure two members are present when they encounter the poor.

By the late nineteenth and early twentieth centuries, SVdP organizations began sprouting up throughout the country, as priests saw the growing lay society as a means for the sanctification of their parishioners. The National Council for the United States was established on November 21, 1915. Today, SVdP is represented in every diocese in the nation and is a presence in one of every five parishes nationally.

After the St. Louis founding, America experienced the Mexican War, the Spanish-American War, World War I and World War II. St. Louis literally became the gateway to the West, and Arizona went from a hot, dusty desert with a few outposts of civilization to a wonderland of air conditioning. Millions of servicemen had trained in the West or had been transported there on their way to San Francisco or San Diego. An unending stream of immigrants transformed Phoenix from a backwater community of a few to one of tens of thousands, then hundreds of thousands, then millions. In 1946, the society that had come to St. Louis from France extended itself into the desert. Yes, SVdP had found its way to St. Mary's Catholic Church in downtown Phoenix, Arizona.

2

THE EARLY YEARS AND
THE STRUGGLE TO SURVIVE

1946 to 1980

During this period, there were four elected St. Vincent de Paul Phoenix (SVdP Phoenix) presidents. In descending order, the first president was Matt Scott, followed by Dan O'Meara, Mort Staub and Joseph Connors. James Finnerty served as the president from 1980 to 1986. He recalled that his immediate predecessor, Staub, put enormous stress on the use of the dining room, and that the man before him, Connors, ate in the dining room every day. "This was the center of his life and served as Connors's virtual office," said Finnerty. The first four presidents have since died and are remembered for their contributions.

A little over one hundred years after the founding of SVdP in the United States, a group of men in Phoenix, Arizona, decided to start SVdP Phoenix. On April 26, 1946, the first conference meeting was held in St. Mary's Church, now the Basilica of St. Mary's, to try and find a solution to the extreme poverty found in Arizona at the time. Father Louis Schoen, OFM (Order of Friars Minor), presided over this formation. Tommy Johnstone, who was from New York; Matt Scott, who worked for the IRS; Dan O'Meara, who worked for a car dealership; Art Whitney; Louis Oliger; and Matt Trudelle were early workers. The first conference president was Matthew Trudelle.

After World War II, the Phoenix area began to grow and prosper, but unfortunately, the levels of poverty grew with it. There were many individuals who were poor or homeless living in or near the downtown Phoenix area.

St. Mary's Basilica, where SVdP Phoenix began.

When SVdP Phoenix began in 1946, many Phoenix residents were living in extreme poverty and living in tents. *Photograph retrieved from the Library of Congress.*

Many were living in tents or just sleeping on the streets. There were also large poor populations living south of Phoenix in the Mexican and Black communities. There was considerable discrimination in early Phoenix, and minorities were forced to live in segregated areas.

Matt Scott and Matthew Trudelle were looking for new members and decided to contact Father Robert Donohue, who was the pastor of St. Agnes Parish, to ask for his assistance. Father Donohue was very supportive in bringing SVdP to Phoenix, and he was given copies of the SVdP manual and other pertinent information. He recommended contacting V.G. "Pete" Barabe, P.P. Stephens and Philip Lusson from St. Agnes Parish and J. Ray Brown and Louis Heil from St. Francis Xavier Parish. Ray Brown had been a member of SVdP in Dubuque, Iowa, and had brought needed perspective to the conference. All the men joined St. Mary's Conference. Other recruits who joined the fledging conference included Wilbur Bluhme, George Chiles, Clem Cruz, Ed Harrington, Cletus Hipskind, Tony Laur, Mickey McGinn, Jim Suffolk and Tom Suffolk.

In its early years, St. Mary's Conference took calls from all over the valley, from South Mountain to North Mountain and from Glendale to Tempe. Most of the calls for assistance were forwarded to the conference by the parish receptionists or directly from priests who knew of SVdP Phoenix. After operating for over a year, members from St. Agnes and St. Francis Xavier parishes decided to break away and start their own conferences.

There was a small conference located in the nearby mining town of Miami, Arizona, about one hundred miles east of Phoenix. It was started in 1948 at Blessed Sacrament Parish; the pastor and spiritual advisor was Father Cornelius Moynihan. This early conference, however, never became part of SVdP Phoenix.

It should be noted that, in those days, St. Mary's occupied a very special place within the Diocese of Tucson in an area that eventually became the Diocese of Phoenix. In 1946, the population of Tucson was larger than the population of Phoenix, and Phoenix was located about one hundred miles north of Tucson. The Franciscan Pastors of St. Mary's were answerable to their order and were far away from the more influential religious voices in the Phoenix area. But they were always respectful of the authority of the Bishop of Tucson. Only in extreme cases did Tucson ever presume to dictate to Phoenix, though they did at least once, when, in the late 1940s, the St. Mary's Conference mishandled a racially charged incident involving admissions into St. Mary's schools.

Still, St. Mary's was a Franciscan church and, hence, was somewhat independent, since Franciscans are a religious order with their own government. Already devoted to the poor and with numerous missions to the indigenous population, St. Mary's was already the founder of many valley institutions, including two St. Mary's grade schools, one for English-speaking students and one for Spanish-speaking students (by 1946, only the English-speaking school was still in existence). They also operated a girls' and a boys' high school. A convent for the Sisters of the Precious Blood, who taught in the St. Mary's schools, stood across Fourth Street, facing Monroe Street. Until 1928, every Catholic church in Maricopa County began as a mission of St. Mary's. Surrounded by Catholic institutions, St. Mary's indeed operated as a sort of autonomous fiefdom, as Tucson was so far away, and there is reason to believe that the founders, like Matt Scott and Dan O'Meara, probably thought that SVdP in Phoenix would always operate with St. Mary's as its base of operations.

In September 1948, Father Victor Bucher, OFM, succeeded Father Louis Schoen, OFM, as the pastor of St. Mary's Parish. Father Victor had been very active with SVdP in Seattle, Washington, and Oakland, California. He became the spiritual advisor for St. Mary's Conference and urged each of the other conferences to apply for aggregation so that, with three aggregated conferences, they could form a particular council.

As recommended by Father Victor Bucher, St. Mary's Conference made a formal application for aggregation to the Paris headquarters through the national office in New York City. St. Mary's Conference received its official aggregation notice with a formation date of August 1949. St. Francis Xavier also received an aggregation notice with a formation date of August 1949. St. Agnes Conference forwarded its application to the office of Bishop Daniel J. Gercke in Tucson and received an aggregation notice with a formation date of May 1949. On December 4, 1949, three conferences from St. Agnes, St. Mary and St. Francis Xavier founded a particular council within the Diocese of Tucson. It became a separate particular council when the Diocese of Phoenix was formed in 1969. The first officers of the new council were Matt Scott, president; Mickey McGinn, vice president; Peter Stephens, secretary; and Dan O'Meara, treasurer. The three conferences identified were from the three largest parishes in Phoenix, and they were all located in what was then considered central Phoenix.

Also located in central Phoenix were the Immaculate Heart of Mary, St. Matthew, St. Anthony and the newly formed St. Mark Parishes. The population of Phoenix was under ninety thousand at the time, and it consisted of seventeen square miles. Even before SVdP Phoenix was established, the parishes all had a "poor box," which collected money to help the poor. The amount of money collected was always small, but it did provide a dedicated source of funding. It was a hand-to-mouth existence. O'Meara later remembered, "Often times, we wouldn't have the money in the treasury to cover the meals, so we all dug in our pockets and always had enough to cover it and a little left over to help with the next week." The religious individuals involved with the founding of this particular council included Monsignor Robert Donahoe, Father Cornelius Moynihan, Father James Deasey, S.J., and Most Revered Reverend Francis J. Green, the Bishop of Tucson. Father Charles Hackel of the Archdiocese of San Francisco also assisted; the first conference was established in San Francisco in 1860.

Shortly after the formation of the Phoenix Particular Council, the Most Revered Daniel J. Gercke, the Bishop of Tucson, appointed Father Victor as the spiritual advisor of the newly created particular council. Matt Scott served as the president until 1965, with Dan O'Meara succeeding him through 1968. Joseph Connors, who had been an SVdP member for twelve years, served as president until 1974, and Mort Staub served until 1980.

Today, the membership of SVdP Phoenix is heavily populated by senior citizens. Understandably, it is difficult for families with young children to

Matt and Helene Scott and their six children: Father Joel, Sister Matthew Mary, Patricia, Marion, Cecelia and Teresa Ann. *Photograph courtesy of Patricia Rush.*

From left to right: Glennie Scott, Matt Scott, Peggy O'Meara and Dan O'Meara. Both men remarried after the deaths of their first wives.

volunteer their time to serve; most of their time is dedicated to work and to the issues related with raising a young family. But in 1946, both Matt Scott and Dan O'Meara, who were both working and raising young families, found the time to start SVdP Phoenix. Scott and his wife, Helena, who was known as "Gippy," had six children; O'Meara and his wife, Mel, had one child. There is no doubt that raising a young family, holding a full-time job and managing this growing organization was not easy. The children of both of these men spoke highly of their fathers and told of how these men found the time to raise them and generously provide for the needs of their young families. It was a balancing act to find time to be a good father while working to address the serious poverty problem found throughout the state of Arizona, more specifically in Phoenix.

Both Matt Scott and Dan O'Meara were considered iconic symbols of SVdP Phoenix and served as mentors for younger members. Both men lost their first wives, who were actively involved whenever possible. Both men remarried after the deaths of their spouses: Scott married Glennie and O'Meara married Peggy. As if by divine intervention, both women became strong supporters and continued serving with SVdP Phoenix until their deaths. Both men dedicated the rest of their lives to the organization.

In the society's early days, Matt Scott and the others would meet in St. Mary's old rectory, which was first built in 1897 and then demolished by Father Victor Bucher in 1948. After that, they met in the new rectory, which is still standing. Scott's daughter, Barb Rush, remembers her father attending meetings at 7:00 p.m. every Tuesday evening, where members passed the hat, a practice that continues to this day. Funding was relatively primitive, with donations accepted and occasional mass collections taken. She also recalls

Thrift store manager Sam Lew and Sister Roqueta Zappia.

her father attending national meetings in New York and giving lectures in Douglas and Bisbee, Arizona.

At a special meeting held at St. Mary's on April 20, 1950, the decision was made to establish a thrift store, and a one-year lease on a small building located at 730 East Washington Street was signed for $75.00 per month. Louis Oliger was appointed chairman of the thrift store committee, and $200.00 (of the treasury's $437.82) was transferred from the treasury to the committee. The new store was opened on May 1, 1950. On September 14, 1950, a second store was opened at 419 East Washington Street with rent at $175.00 per month for the first six months and then $200.00 for the last six months. On September 18, 1951, a warehouse was leased at 2108 West Buckeye Road for two years at $150 per month. During this early period, SVdP Phoenix also ran a thrift store and a warehouse at the corner of Fifth Avenue and Madison Street, which were managed by Sam Lew.

Henry F. Unger remembered the humble beginnings of one of SVdP Phoenix's signature programs, feeding the hungry: "Every day of the week, the needy would ring the bell at the Church of St. Mary's...to beg for food. Facilities were lacking and only sandwiches could be distributed."

Vincentians, under Father Victor's instigation, found a small deserted restaurant, previously known as Johnny's Restaurant, at 435 West Washington Street. With dining-area seating for thirty-six individuals, this space became the first SVdP Phoenix dining room on November 20, 1952, with John Bedway as its manager. The rent was one hundred dollars per month, but a generous anonymous benefactor donated the rent money. It was revealed many years later that the benefactor was a member of SVdP Phoenix named William Wasson. Only twenty-three people came to the opening.

Henry Unger recalled that Vincentians used their own cars and trucks on weekends to gather up unwanted vegetables from nearby fields for the restaurant. Matt Scott remembered:

> *One fall day, a farmer told us he had cabbage we could pick. Art Whitney and I got in Art's truck and headed for the field to pick what turned out to be a ton of cabbage. Tired but thankful, we jumped in the truck with*

On November 20, 1952, SVdP Phoenix purchased Johnny's Restaurant (seating capacity of thirty-six), located at 435 West Washington Street, Phoenix, Arizona.

Chief cook and dining room manager John Bedway.

the cabbage and realized we were stuck in the field due to our ambitious load. By the time we unloaded, got the truck to drier ground and loaded up again, we knew that we had done a day's work, but John was able to make wonderful soups, stews and coleslaw for quite some time, so it was well worth it.

Demand soon escalated, and John Bedway, the manager and cook, donated his services for virtually nothing, saying, "God will take care of those who help the poor." Cletus Hipskind recalled, "Depending on the number of hungry folks that appeared, John Bedway's stew might well be stretched to become soup to ensure everyone was fed." But the building had two problems: it was too small, and the growing lines of poor awaiting service disturbed other merchants. In 1954, the dining room was moved to the corner of Ninth Avenue and Madison Street, where it could seat four hundred people, until 1960, when the dining room was expanded to hold more people. The Washington Street stores were also moved to this new location. On February 25, 1957, the executive board recommended the purchase of the building located at 814 West Madison Street, next door to the dining room. The recommendation was approved, and the building was purchased for $10,765.

Matt Scott began his work in a city of about one hundred thousand that was emerging from, first, the Great Depression, in which thousands of homes had been foreclosed, and then World War II, which had convulsed most of the world and left everyone wondering if the peace would lead to another downturn in the national economy. There was little reason to anticipate the super growth that was to ensue.

The 1950s were a time of overall growth for Phoenix, with the population going up about 300 percent. Father Warren Rousse later wrote, "The Society also performed traditional works of charity. Members visited poor families and helped out in any way they could. They fed the hungry and attempted to find shelter for those that came to St. Mary's church for help,

Clients waiting in line to be served. SVdP Phoenix dining room, located at 119 South Ninth Avenue.

gave coupons for free haircuts and tried to find permanent and temporary jobs for the unemployed." In 1965, SVdP Phoenix began a holiday tradition of providing Christmas and Thanksgiving meals.

At a June 11, 1965 meeting, the board of directors passed a resolution on the tenure of its president. "Resolved: That the President of the Particular Council of Maricopa County be elected to a term of office consisting of three years, and may serve no more than two such three-year terms in succession. The term of office to begin on October first, the beginning of the Society's year." After a short discussion, the motion was passed unanimously. At the same meeting, Dan O'Meara was elected president. That same year, Matt Scott became the president of the Central Council for the Diocese of Tucson.

In 1966, the first quarterly magazine, the *Vincentian*, was published. The dedication shown by SVdP Phoenix members had allowed the organization to continue expanding. Through the efforts of journalist Henry Unger, word of the kitchen spread. Unger, a reporter, served as the publicity man for St. Vincent de Paul. "No one understands how important Henry Unger was," said Jim Novotny, a longtime Vincentian. The movement gained the outside world's attention when Walter Cronkite and John Chancellor aired national stories on CBS and NBC. Years later, the *Vincentian* described what had become a typical scene outside the old dining hall:

> *Patiently, the often ragged and poorly dressed will stand or sit along Madison Avenue, up South 9th Avenue, and around Jefferson Avenue. Many will be depressed, lonely, unemployed, sickly, elderly. For many, a tiny pension or a minimum Social Security payment helped eke out some lodging and some necessities of life. For others, there is starvation without the dinner at the charity. Children, disheveled, gaunt and dirty-faced, cling to their equally gaunt-looking parents. It is difficult to explain to them why they must stand in this line, hoping for a decent meal. Unable to understand unemployment and the hard life, the children, irritable because of their hunger, wriggle, cry, and irritate others with similar problems.*

In 1967, a thief jimmied a window open and stole into the charity dining room, stealing twenty-five dozen eggs and some four hundred pounds of prepared meat. He left behind a broken whisky bottle, two quarters and a lighter. Donations balanced out the loss, and the service continued.

The dining room on Madison Street virtually became holy ground for a generation of Vincentians who called it "the Miracle on Madison

Street." A November 1969 article in the *Vincentian* described its process of food preparation:

> *Long before the hungry poor move into the dining room daily, preparations occur behind the scenes. Our driver makes the rounds, picking up food from generous donors; our cooks and helpers peel vegetables, arrange food to be cooked on trays, check food cooking in large pots and in the large oven. Every effort is made to provide protein-vitamin full dinners for the diners. All is geared to be served promptly for the 11:30 a.m. opening time every day of the week. There is joy when a generous supply of food is received and sadness when the intake is lean. All is done in a clean, modern kitchen, where cooking equipment has been donated. Even food trays are thoroughly scalded and washed. Menus vary from day to day because the cook never knows how much and what kind of food will be available.*

Growth continued throughout the 1960s and 1970s, despite a sputtering national economy crippled by the Vietnam War. By 1965, SVdP in Arizona consisted of twenty-five parish conferences with more than two hundred members. This was accomplished through the tireless efforts of the extension committee, which consisted of Joe Barabe, Ray Brown, Joe Connors, Dan O'Meara, Bill Shiels and Matt Scott, who traversed the state from Flagstaff to Douglas between 1950 and 1969, setting up new conferences of charity, which have always been the backbone of the society. Conference work carried on in a confidential manner to preserve the dignity of those who receive assistance. For this reason, it has often been called the "Silent Society."

Ten drop boxes permeated the valley, and once or twice a week, SVdP Phoenix members visited them and brought the contents to the store located at Fifth Avenue and Madison Street. The drop boxes were sponsored by donors who had their names placed on the boxes; they cost about eighty-five dollars each. During this early period, five thrift stores were open, sometimes holding collectable treasures that hobbyists wanted. There were unusual spoons, rare books, dolls, old shoes, irons and other items at the thrift store, "where the visitor may browse to their heart's content and where they could buy items at low costs." Even the rising hippie generation came to buy beads.

Though women had long been active as volunteers for SVdP, it was not until 1969 that the national SVdP invited them to become members. Times were changing, and SVdP changed with them.

In November 1973, SVdP Phoenix began the construction of an addition to the dining room that was meant to include administrative space, a kitchen and storage area of 5,100 square feet and improve the feeding capacity of the dining room. "We have been operating on a shoestring for about eighteen years in the present building with the structure inadequate for the mounting numbers of hungry we are feeding," said Mort Staub, the chairman of the dining room committee and the vice president at the time. "Our lines of needy have increased considerably and we were working with the equipment held together by Scotch Tape and string. Typical examples were turkeys donated by people which had to be boned days ahead of the cooking because only old pizza ovens with small space were available." The new facility added 600 square feet of centralized freezer space. Previously, there had been only 128. Eight tons of refrigeration equipment was installed.

But this was the era of stagflation, both higher prices and drastically higher unemployment, which was not supposed to be possible and baffled a decade of political leadership. Even the employed found their buying power steadily lowered. "Our facility has become a sort of barometer for the financial situation in the greater Phoenix area," said Joseph C. Kostolnik, the dining room manager, "and based on the great numbers of needy coming to our doors, it isn't completely good." In November 1974, the *Vincentian* reported that, in the previous summer, the hungry poor had not declined in number as they usually did in the hot summer, and as a result, food stocks had almost been depleted, forcing the closure of the dining hall doors for the first time in twenty-two years. Kostolnik said:

> *We managed to weather through these difficult summer months, but we are already becoming concerned about the much heavier feeding fall and winter periods. Particularly, we are worried about enough food for our big, traditional Thanksgiving and Christmas dinners, when we normally serve nearly 3,000 turkey dinners and the trimmings, when our doors open far beyond our daily feeding periods so that everyone receives the holiday dinner.*

As SVdP philosophy dating back to Frederic Ozaman has it, "No work of charity is foreign to the society." Its efforts tend to naturally ramify into related fields and are limited only by resources, will and imagination. In 1977, a free medical and dental clinic was created at the site of the Madison Street and Ninth Avenue dining room with the help of Vincentian Sal Immordino. Dr. Max Lieberman, DDS, founded the clinic and became the first volunteer dentist. In the early days, service was limited to emergency dental aid, which often consisted of just pulling out a bad tooth. This was the forerunner of today's more sophisticated efforts in different places. Mary Ann Baranowski remembered:

> *The medical and dental clinic was located at Ninth Avenue and Madison when I began volunteering as a clerk in the 1980s. We served the homeless and poor who were unable to afford assistance, those seriously affected by the recession of the 1980s, and some of the people who fled for their lives from certain Central and South American countries.*

Basic services were offered because SVdP Phoenix had only one medical room and one dental room with two dental chairs. There were no appointments; a person who called was advised the morning the doctor or dentist was volunteering, and services were provided on a first-come, first-served basis for a maximum of six to eight patients per day. For the most part, dental work was limited to extractions and occasional fillings, though, for a time, patients could obtain dentures at a very low cost. A gentleman once came in wearing shoes that were too small for his feet and no socks, so he had a number of sores and blisters on his feet. The doctor had the patient cleaned and treated his feet. The society obtained a couple of pairs of socks and properly sized shoes from the ministry and gave them to the homeless man as he left, walking gingerly but happily.

One of SVdP Phoenix's strongest supporters, Rabbi Albert Plotkin. *Photograph courtesy of Arizona Jewish Historical Society, Pearl and Cecil Newmark Memorial Archives.*

SVdP Phoenix's very approach dictated that there would be many fronts. In 1978, the increasing needs of the poor and homeless, coupled with the increasing generosity of valley residents, prompted the society to move to a forty-thousand-square-foot warehouse that had been erected at 3333 East Elwood Street in Phoenix. The larger facility greatly helped with the storage and delivery of furniture, clothing and household goods for those in need. The number of thrift stores increased from one in 1950 to an array of stores located throughout the Diocese of Phoenix today. Outstanding interfaith aid was extended on Christmas by volunteers from Temple Beth

Israel, who said, "We want to give the Christians a day off at Christmas." Each year, volunteers served the poor, while Rabbi Albert Plotkin presented both Christian and Jewish holiday carols. During this period, the stores, resources and twinning committees were started, and they remain stable and viable committees today.

3

THE YEARS OF GROWTH

1980 to 1990

During the ten years between 1980 and 1990, three elected presidents and their respective boards of directors served, with James Finnerty being elected three times; he served his first term from 1980 to 1983, his second term from 1983 to 1986 and his third term from 1989 to 1990. Ron Meyer served from 1986 to 1989. It was a time of growth, a time of introducing new ideas and a time of strong leadership. Several professionals from outside St. Vincent de Paul Phoenix were brought in to work with the society's members. This included Jim Gallagher, a partner at Price Waterhouse; Ron Meyer, an attorney; and William Dunn, a local physician. When this period began in 1980, there were no district councils and all parish conferences made up the Maricopa Particular Council's general membership.

In 1982, the SVdP Phoenix Board of Directors created an executive director position, hiring David Bratton as the first executive director. Two years later, Gary Brown became the executive director and served until his retirement in 1989. Gary returned to serve as a member of the board of directors.

In 1980, the Maricopa Particular Council first hosted a national convention, beginning of a new chapter of its life. By 1980, some thirty years of determination and sweat had turned the Vincentians from a few laymen scrabbling from hand-to-mouth with practically no resources into a large-scale organization serving thousands of people across Arizona. Yet, despite the many achievements of this heroic age, SVdP Phoenix was weak in organization and structure. The founding Vincentians were familiar with

Gary Brown served as SVdP Phoenix executive director from 1984 to 1989, followed by service on the board of directors.

the society's rules and procedures, and for many years, its smallness had kept people on the same page; now, it was getting too large for that. The society also faced the subtle threat of complacency, of people being satisfied with maintaining their own comfort zone. It is difficult for people who have known each other and worked together for decades to entertain new ideas. Some new volunteers were calling themselves Vincentians while working under very little central control. Innocent of breaking the most basic rules, such as always visiting the poor face to face in their homes, they were, at times, unobserved by members who did not know or care to know the rules. Volunteers who did not work for a salary could not simply be ordered to do things a certain way. Even worse, those outside Phoenix sometimes resented what they saw as heavy-handed direction from a central authority ignorant of local conditions.

Finnerty began volunteering with SVdP Phoenix in 1967, first under Connors and then Staub. In 1968, he became treasurer, and in 1980, he was elected president. He decided that the board needed young blood to breathe new life into the organization. SVdP Phoenix was responding to community needs by becoming more professional. It was important to establish guidelines for the role of Vincentians so that everyone was serving in the same manner. The idea was "to inculcate rules and get more professionals into the society," Finnerty said. "Every conference was doing things their own way, applying their own interpretations of the rules."

Once a month or so, the Ozanam School held voluntary classes covering various functions of serving as a Vincentian; while attending the classes was strictly voluntary, they served as the beginning of change. Ron Meyer, who also supported mandatory education, followed Jim Finnerty as president. It wasn't until the presidency of Steve Jenkins, however, that rules were finalized, requiring the completion of classes prior to serving as an officer; they were later required to become a member. This, in time, eliminated any legitimate excuse for not following the rules.

Gary Brown, who had served as the executive director, remembered the society's warehouse located on Thirty-Second and Elwood Streets. SVdP Phoenix had sold the warehouse to the developer of the Southbank development. The warehouse was located in the proposed gateway of the development, and the purchase provided SVdP Phoenix with enough seed money to build its current Watson Road location.

SVdP Phoenix purchased the Watkins property from a national trucking firm because of its close proximity to the city, the I-17 Freeway and its previous use as a truckyard and warehouse. Brown and the warehouse manager visited St. Vincent de Paul, Salvation Army and other facilities in cities up and down the West Coast to develop plans for the new facility. One feature that stood out to them was the chapel at a Los Angeles facility that was available for use by employees. While a chapel could not be included on the society's initial campus, an outdoor gathering area was created, complete with a canopy that resembled a chapel roof. The initial plans for the campus included a conference training center, administrative offices and a fifty-thousand-square-foot warehouse. Long-range plans included a chapel, outdoor restrooms, an orchard and garden and a central dining room and food processing center.

In 1982, a group of men from Our Lady of Perpetual Help (OLPH) Parish, located in Scottsdale, created an annual food drive to help St. Vincent de Paul. Rom Caroselli was the first president of the newly formed group, which received strong support from then-Bishop Thomas O'Brien and OLPH pastor Monsignore Eugene Maguire. In 1982, it was agreed that the men of OLPH would establish a food bank and initiate a food drive for Thanksgiving of that year. The kickoff was held at OLPH, starting with mass and followed by breakfast. Jim Novotny, a Vincentian and member of the OLPH Parish, helped organize these initial efforts and continued working on subsequent food drives. Within a few years, this became an annual event, with other parishes joining the effort, including the celebration of mass, breakfast and the distribution of supplies for the food drive. The Bel Canto Choir (directed by Jeanne Dearing) provided music. Eddie Basha, the president of Bashas' grocery stores, attended and donated funds to provide grocery bags to conferences throughout the valley.

Eventually, up to seventy-five parishes participated, and a spring food drive was also initiated. In 2018, about thirty-five thousand bags of food and over $100,000 in donations were collected, filling SVdP Phoenix pantries. Since 1982, it is estimated that this single food drive program has resulted in over $50 million donated to purchase food supplies for conferences. More importantly, parishioners at churches are part of this charity work, donating food and participating in the society's mission to help those in need.

Over the years, the men of OLPH; Bishops Thomas Olmsted and Eduardo Nevares; diocesan parish priests; the priests at OLPH, including Monsignore Tom Hever and Father Greg Schlarb; Father Emile Pelletier (and other St. Vincent de Paul spiritual directors); Deacon Tom Phelan; and Vincentians from OLPH, including Ed Tynan, Frank Plona, Richard Childress, Dan Troop, Ed Slezak, Armand Dion and Brian O'Donnell, with assistance from St. Vincent de Paul, have all contributed greatly to the effort.

In 1987, the food bank and warehouse opened on the society's main campus on Watkins Road. The food bank was started out of a five-thousand-square-foot storage area. Jim Winkler was one of the first managers. The new facility provided food to over fifty conferences at that time; the food was either purchased with funds or donated by local grocers.

The food reclamation program officially began with Fry's Food Stores. Members of SVdP Phoenix teamed up with Fry's to reclaim the store's damaged food stocks. Fry's provided the expertise needed to set up the warehouse and trained staff in handling the products that were received. Fry's also provided the scanning equipment and software that was needed to keep track of the products and stores that were sending products. Each item was scanned and recorded by vendor. An invoice detailing each item was produced and mailed to the vendors monthly. After the product had been scanned and recorded, most of the usable product was donated to SVdP Phoenix in exchange for performing the scanning operation. The initial donations in 1988 comprised around one million pounds of nonperishable food items. By the late 1980s, all crates that contained even one dented can were sent straight from the Fry's warehouse to SVdP Phoenix with the proviso that the food could not be sent out of state or sold. A few years ago, Fry's changed its policy so that only dented cans were sent to the society. In 1989, a twenty-four-cubic-foot drive-in freezer was added.

As the 1970s ended, new challenges were presented to the society daily. The number of people in need was growing. The families of those in prison cried out for assistance. The Vincentians responded with new ministries called "special works." The *Vincentian*, in July 1982, reported that the Transient Aid Center (TAC) opened on November 1, 1981, at 1123 North Seventh Street to aid travelers stranded in Phoenix. SVdP Phoenix members interviewed people who had an official referral slip from Catholic churches and other sources. The center's services included emergency food, temporary lodging for one day to a week and gasoline. Efforts were made to ensure that the program was not abused. TAC worked closely with hotels, motels and gas stations. All applications for aid were rechecked. A driver's license and car title were required to receive assistance. The original facility was sold to the federal government, and the land was used

In 1981, SVdP Phoenix opened the Transient Aid Center at 1123 North Seventh Street, Phoenix, Arizona.

In 1985, SVdP Phoenix opened a special ministry service to assist individuals and families with their needs.

for the Seventh Street entrance ramp for the 202 Freeway. The program was relocated to a new facility on Twelfth Street and eventually moved to the dining room on Watkins Street.

Another special works ministry began in 1985. The Ministry to the Incarcerated and Their Families (MIF) provided emotional and financial assistance to families whose relatives were incarcerated. SVdP Phoenix members would often visit imprisoned individuals. This function would later include the Ministry to the Recently Released (MRR), in which members would work with prisoners who had been released from prison and their families.

SVdP Phoenix was very good at allowing Vincentians, volunteers and staff to work together to develop ministries to serve the poor and the community. Within a short period of time, other special ministries were added to the list of charitable works that did not fall into a standard category of services. In addition to TAC, MIF and MRR, the special ministries of the society include the following services:

MINISTRY TO THE HOMELESS: Members personally interview people seeking housing, clothing, showers, bus tickets and help with acquiring identification. They discuss the desire of the person to get out of homelessness and recommend appropriate actions to them.

FAMILY ASSISTANCE MINISTRY AND CRISIS BILL 200: Members meet face to face with applicants who require help to determine their qualification for assistance, and they assess the amount of assistance that needs to be provided.

St. Anne's Ministry: Members contact applicants by phone to arrange the pick-up of needed appropriate hospital and assistance equipment. They also assist with organizing, sorting and recording the inventory.

Early in the development of special ministries, it was determined a conference might best provide these unique services. As a result, the special ministries were incorporated into a conference in District Seven. In 2006, Joe Power and Ged Walsh applied to have the conference renamed the St. Jude and Pope John Paul II Conference. When the late pope was canonized, the name of the conference was changed to St. John Paul II.

In 1982 and 1983, homelessness was a major problem in Phoenix, and the Vincentians attempted to respond to the growth of the cardboard improvised "cities" (including the original "tent city") by opening a homeless shelter on Ninth Avenue. Jim Finnerty remembered that many people were living under the bridge near Central Avenue. SVdP Phoenix made a one-year commitment to operate a 220-bed temporary emergency shelter; in exchange, the city and business community would develop a plan for people who needed housing. In January 1984, the board of SVdP Phoenix extended its commitment until the end of May. It provided clean beds, shower facilities, a free clothing room, morning and evening meals, toiletries and towels, laundry facilities, a TV room, transportation, alcohol and drug abuse counseling, job referrals and vocational rehabilitation. During this short effort, SVdP Phoenix made use of many volunteers, Vincentians and, yes, even students. Gary Brown remembered how students from Brophy College Preparatory were some of the best volunteers to help serve people in need.

But the homeless shelter was a doomed enterprise. It ceased operations on May 31, 1984, after making arrangements and assisting with contingency plans to relocate its clients to shelters run by the Salvation Army. The *Vincentian* explained that "the emergency shelter had been running since March of 1983…at the time, 550 to 600 homeless persons were living downtown in cardboard and canvas shanties, a situation that was universally decried as deplorable and unsafe." In response to the closing of the SVdP Phoenix shelter, the City of Phoenix created a community committee to help create a new shelter service, which eventually became Central Arizona Shelter Services (CASS). SVdP Phoenix provided CASS with beds and furniture, as well as food for evening snacks.

Despite earlier challenges, SVdP Phoenix did not stop trying to help the homeless crisis, opening Ozanam Manor in 1985. According to Mike Bell, who served as its director from 1988 until 2018, Ozanam Manor is a longer-

Mike Bell speaking with an Ozanam Manor resident. Mike served as the Ozanam Manor director from 1988 to 2018.

term, transitional shelter directed toward the needs of older or disabled homeless people who do not do well in mass emergency (tier I) shelters. It is very hard on them to be required to leave during the day in an area where criminals prey on the most vulnerable, and it is difficult for most of them to find housing quickly by getting a day labor job or other employment.

From its beginning, Ozanam Manor operated as a partnership with local government. The facility—a forty-five-bed disused daycare center, a kitchen and a modified apartment for staff offices—was leased for one dollar a year from the Phoenix Housing Department. The facilities were located at 1730 East Monroe Street in the city's Sidney P. Osborn Housing Community. In 1984, the homeless shelter was opened by the Metropolitan Commission of the United Methodist Church (MEPCO). The director, Poncio Gonzales, whose office was off site, was responsible for several other programs as well. The onsite supervisor, Melody Hicks, was also the lead counselor. The shelter was called tier II because it largely received clients from tier I shelters. The name of the shelter was changed to MEPCO Manor at the request of clients, who thought that name would

Ozanam Manor was established in 1985 at 1730 East Monroe Street, Phoenix, Arizona.

Ozanam Manor residents giving thanks for the assistance and care that they have received at Ozanam Manor.

not tell potential employers that they lived in a homeless shelter. In July 1985, MEPCO decided not to continue with the shelter.

At the time, Arizona's government badly wanted MEPCO's services to continue. The state government agreed that if SVdP Phoenix would take over the shelter, it would be willing to acquire some of the expenses. Some board members had wanted "to stay with what [the society does] best—meals and stores" and pointed out that government grants might create dependency. Influenced largely by the leadership of Dan O'Meara, Jim Finnerty and Gary Brown, and due to the community need, SVdP Phoenix acquired the facility in July and renamed the shelter Ozanam Manor, after St. Vincent de Paul founder Frederic Ozanam. Over the years, Ozanam Manor has received increased government support for operations, including pass-through federal funding contracted with Arizona and Phoenix, as well as a later contract with the U.S. Department of Veterans Affairs. Funding also later came from United Way, the Order of Malta, the BHHS Legacy Foundation and a number of other private sources, along with continuing support from SVdP Phoenix membership. Residents stay at Ozanam Manor for six months on average and may stay for a maximum of two years as their lives stabilize, and steady income is established from employment, Social Security or veterans' benefits. More than two-thirds of Ozanam Manor's residents find permanent housing and become self-sustaining.

Over the years, Ozanam Manor has benefited greatly from being part of SVdP Phoenix, which assists with its administrative functions and connects the program with highly qualified staff and volunteers, including Murray Gibson, a retired corporate lawyer who assisted with program management for many years, volunteers from the Order of Malta, Jesuit and AmeriCorps volunteers and Arizona State University social work interns. Some of the interns have become excellent case managers. With its caring staff, volunteers and a supportive community, Ozanam Manor has been a success.

Gary Brown remembered several donors of the era, especially Eddie Basha. The main donors were grocery stores, Brown said, and many stores donated dented cans, but not Basha's. "I'll never give you a dented can," stated Eddie Basha, and he never did. When asked to take a more public role in his efforts and draw media attention to his business, he answered that he did not want his actions to be seen as advertising because he was doing this for God. Brown also remembered Joe Garagiola's generosity to SVdP Phoenix and stated that he never forgot the society. At one of the society's early fundraising breakfasts, Brown remembered that Joe Garagiola was

John Hook and Kari Lake from Fox 10 News, photographed with Eddie Basha during one of SVdP Phoenix's food drives.

so moved by the presentation made by a former Ozanam Manor resident named Sandy that he spontaneously began asking for donations from those attending. In a relatively short time, Joe raised $188,000 for Ozanam Manor, which, at the time, was the only homeless shelter in Arizona for the elderly and physically or mentally disabled. Other major donors included Discount Tire and Charles Keating; in one year, they combined to donate $1 million.

Ronald Meyer served as SVdP Phoenix's president from 1986 to 1989; he had previously served as legal counsel from 1978 to 1986. He also thought that SVdP Phoenix needed more legal organization and was ready to move it in a new direction. His first order of business was to establish stronger rules for SVdP Phoenix, the heart of which is the Vincentians serving in parish conferences, and completely reorganize. The challenge was to develop an organization that maintained the influence of the individual conference members while, at the same time, it developed an organization wherein special works, which was also important in providing assistance to the poor beyond resources available to many conferences, could be developed and expanded. To accomplish this goal, Meyer developed bylaws that provided that SVdP Phoenix would be divided into ten districts, with each district comprised of six to eight conferences. All special works came under SVdP Phoenix.

The members elected a president who formed a board of directors, which consisted of the presidents of each of the district councils and individuals appointed by the president in a number that could not exceed the number of presidents of the districts. The rules and regulations for the various special works were drafted. Each special works had its own organization. Procedures were made to provide for accountability and compliance with various governmental regulations concerning personnel, food storage, food preparation, et cetera, were put in place. A committee was formed to create and implement the goals and the mission of SVdP Phoenix. A regular program of longterm planning was initiated.

While Meyer was president, the first part of the Watkins Center was built; it included the administrative offices and the warehouse. In 1987, the Watkins Road complex was built on almost ten acres; it housed the warehouse, Vincentian Hall, the chapel and administration offices. The Matthew J. Scott Vincentian Hall was dedicated on June 6 of that year. Plans were soon made to develop the property further with a central kitchen, family dining room, clinic and special works center.

SVdP Phoenix's conferences increased from forty-four to fifty-eight in 1988 as the Vincentian ideal spread. A reclamation center was established so that discarded food from grocery chains could be received, stored and distributed. A large freezer was built to house perishables. The food was then redistributed to conferences that would further distribute it to people in need. A facility that received donations, such as clothing, furniture, et cetera, was also established. Items could be repaired and then distributed to the various stores. The number of thrift stores was expanded to increase revenues and provide a place where conferences could send clients to obtain clothing, furniture and household goods. A system of "twinning" was also established wherein the wealthier conferences would have a means to provide money to the poorer conferences. In addition to the OLPH Food Drive Breakfast, an annual breakfast was established as a fundraiser. The first breakfast was attended by about 100 people at the dining room. Now, 1,400 guests attend the breakfast, which is held at a local resort each fall, raising over $1 million each year.

On April 17, 1989, SVdP Phoenix decided to expand its established recycling program to include glass, paper, cardboard, aluminum, rags, metals and plastics. The City of Phoenix made the program possible when it made SVdP Phoenix the sole recipient of all recyclables from its pilot recycling project. Then–executive director Gary Brown was appreciative: "We are extremely thankful to the City of Phoenix. The society has been actively searching for ways to increase income, as monetary donations have been dwindling. The revenue generated from this program should help our organization considerably." The city distributed blue barrels to four thousand target homes and arranged for a weekly pick-up schedule, delivering recyclables to SVdP Phoenix daily. It was anticipated that 2,500 tons of recyclable material would be delivered over a twelve-month period, producing $130,000 in revenue. Today, SVdP Phoenix is no longer in the recycling business.

While SVdP Phoenix was generally run by volunteers, a core of professional staff was needed. Under the direction of then–executive director Gary Brown, a professional staff of accountants and fundraisers, a human resource manager, food service director, et cetera, was created. At the end of Ron Meyer's term, a legal structure was put in place that facilitated and encouraged the involvement of individual Vincentians in the work of SVdP Phoenix and provided the means for special works to grow and expand. A capital campaign was initiated to develop the remaining portion of the Watkins Center to include a large central kitchen and a family dining room, a medical clinic and facilities for expanding special works to assist families, traveler's aid, et cetera.

Steve Jenkins photographed in Cuernavaca, Mexico. Steve started the partnership between Cuernavaca and SVdP Phoenix.

During this period, led by future president Steve Jenkins, the first sister conference was established in Cuernavaca, Mexico. Jenkins remembered staying with a family in Cuernavaca as a student studying Spanish in 1987. He had discussed his experiences as a member of SVdP's St. Gregory Conference in Phoenix. After the discussion, the father of the family, Emil Taboada, requested that Jenkins send him information on SVdP Phoenix. On receiving and reading the information, Taboada talked to his parish priest, Father Baltazar Bucio, and the two agreed to start an SVdP conference in the parish in Cuernavaca.

Calls to serve with SVdP were made at the Sunday masses, and a new conference, St. John the Evangelist Conference, was formed in April 1988. A few months later, Jenkins invited Taboada to Phoenix to visit SVdP Phoenix's various ministries and experience how they operated. Taboada came to Phoenix in April 1989 and stayed for a week. Before returning to Cuernavaca, Taboada requested and received funds from SVdP Phoenix to start a medical clinic in his parish as part of the SVdP work there. Taboada's experience in Phoenix and written material on SVdP Phoenix provided him with the structure of the society that he needed in Cuernavaca. Jenkins and Taboada began a partnership that provided the basis for the relationship between Phoenix and Cuernavaca.

The first conference began operations in St. John the Evangelist (San Juan Evangelista) Church. The church had unused rooms on its property at the time, and the conference was able to start a small thrift store, provide medical and dental services, store commodities for home visits and use workshops to fabricate arts and crafts for additional sales in the thrift store. During this time, two more conferences were added, one near St. John's and the other at the Cathedral of Cuernavaca. There were several members, and the programs for families and elderly people increased. However, after about three years, the San Juan Evangelista Parish Church needed additional space for its programs, and SVdP moved the medical and dental clinics to a space that was provided by the family of one of its members. Within four years, there were five conferences forming a particular council. Years later, the council was incorporated as the Society of St. Vincent de Paul Council of the State of Morelos (SVdP Morelos).

In 1989, an important program of SVdP Morelos was initiated, which helped cement the bond between members in Cuernavaca and Phoenix. Taboada was so impressed with the work in Phoenix that he wanted Cuernavaca Vincentians to visit Phoenix and begin to understand the structure and operations there. Jenkins also needed local assistance to provide support to the conferences in Cuernavaca. Taboada and Jenkins started a program called *intercambio* in which members of both communities would visit the other, and over the years, strong ties would develop. Between 1989 and 2019, there have been eighty-eight visitors to Cuernavaca from Phoenix and other states and forty-four visitors to Phoenix from Cuernavaca. In total, there have been 135 trips to Cuernavaca, not including the visits every six months by Jenkins.

In the initial years of home visits, the members began to realize that a major cause for the cycle of poverty within the families was the tendency of children to drop out of school—many times due to the lack of resources required to attend school. Although there is free public education through high school, many families still cannot afford to send children to school because of the costs of school supplies, clothing, books and transportation. In 1991, the conferences adopted six students and began providing financial and other assistance to them with the purpose of keeping them in school as long as possible. In time, other individuals began to donate scholarships (*becas*) to students. This practice has grown through the assistance of individual donors and now helps 120 students. Individual sponsors in Phoenix and other parts of the United States provide eighty-five students with becas, and individuals in Cuernavaca provide an additional forty-five becas.

Students from Cuernavaca, Mexico, recipients of SVdP Phoenix scholarships.

In 1990, another program initiated by the Conference of the Asuncion de Maria assisted fifty elderly persons each month with a food box called *despensa de alieamentos* or *despensa*. This function was taken over by SVdP Cuernavaca and now serves both elderly persons and families with over three hundred despensas monthly.

4

MAJOR ACCOMPLISHMENTS

1990 to 1996

The only elected president during this period was Terry B. Wilson, who not only served honorably as president but later also served on the St. Vincent de Paul Board of Directors for both the national and international councils. Bob Bosler became executive director in March 1991 and retired in the spring of 1996. Bosler was a longtime Vincentian who told stories of how, when he was a child, he would accompany his father on visits to assist the poor. Bosler was a retired air force colonel and did an excellent job as executive director. Chris Becker, who had been employed as the director of operations and food services since 1987, was promoted to executive director when Bosler retired. Unfortunately, a tragic accident occurred at his home on September 8, 1996; he was electrocuted and died at the age of forty-six. The SVdP Phoenix Sunnyslope Chris Becker Memorial Dining Room bears his name.

One of the most important SVdP Phoenix staff functions provided today comes from Vincentian Support Services. During this period, this service was initially called Conference Support, and in 1997, the name was changed to Vincentian Support Services, as the staff members were providing support to Vincentians at all levels, not just those in the conferences. John Feit was the first head of this department and served admirably during this period. In simple terms, the main function of this service was to assist conferences and Vincentians in whatever way possible to make their jobs easier, to act as a positive resource and to assist members with meeting their spiritual and regulatory requirements.

Above: Terry Wilson, SVdP Phoenix president from 1990 to 1996, and Bob Bosler, executive director from 1991 to 1996.

Left: Chris Becker served as executive director from the spring of 1996 until his premature death in September 1996 at the age of forty-six.

In 1990, land was purchased to house the Mesa Dining Room. Wilson remembered that SVdP Phoenix needed $160,000 to keep the dining room open. He approved the expenditure on a Friday, though there was no money. Over the weekend, a $162,000 bequest was received. Wilson still does not seem surprised at the windfall: "Things like that happened all the time," he said.

The Dan O'Meara Center was built on a little over nine acres of property in 1987 at a cost of $965,000, including closing costs. It was a central location that housed the warehouse, administration offices and Vincentian chapel. The architect for the Dan O'Meara Center was Maret Webb, who would later design the new Ozanam Manor and Resource Center, which opened in May 2018. The Dan O'Meara Center dedication, however, did not occur until November 25, 1991. The center, which housed the central kitchen and family dining room, was officially dedicated at 420 West Watkins Road. The keynote speaker was campaign chairman Eddie Basha. Also in attendance were Bishop Thomas J. O'Brien; Reverend Vincent J. Nevulis, Spiritual Advisor of SVdP Phoenix; the Honorable Paul Johnson, mayor; Mary Rose Wilcox, city councilwoman for District Seven; Calvin Goode, city councilman for District Eight; and Mary Jo West, broadcast journalist. SVdP Phoenix board president Terry Wilson, Bishop O'Brien and campaign chairman Eddie Basha had broken ground for the special works area in 1987.

During this period, a funding program called Campaign for Caring was initiated. The campaign was a major effort that aimed to raise $2.5 million to replace the dilapidated charity dining room located at Ninth Avenue and Madison Street. The *Vincentian* magazine wrote, "People from the local community, such as Eddie Basha, Earl Katz, Burton Barr, Pamela Grant, Fritz Rentschler and Bob Russell, worked long and hard as the core group for our capital campaign. They are still working to solicit pledges and contributions to bring us to our 2.5-million-dollar goal."

The campaign received support from then-governor Rose Mofford, who signed a proclamation declaring a Campaign for Caring Week. The faith-based community response was overwhelming, and the following religious institutions became personally involved in the campaign: American Baptist Church, Episcopal Diocese of Arizona, First Institutional Baptist Church, North Phoenix Baptist Church, St. George Eastern Orthodox Church, Temple Kol Ami, United Methodist Church and the Catholic Diocese of Phoenix. The religious leaders from these institutions had already asked their congregations to contribute financially to the charity dining room; then, they showed up at SVdP Phoenix to personally serve the poor. This was truly a moment of interfaith collaboration.

Eddie Basha's efforts on behalf of the poor continued after this spectacular fundraising drive—this time, with the holiday food drive. The Bashas' stores throughout the area served as food donation points. Bashas' challenged the public to donate by pledging to match up to one hundred food units. KPNX-TV 12 promoted the food drive through station public service announcements, and KNIX-FM launched the drive with a remote broadcast at a Bashas' store by station personality John Michaels.

In SVdP Phoenix's formative years, little was needed in terms of financial planning and analysis because the members of the first conferences depended on donations on an as-needed or as-available basis, and financial analysis or advanced planning was simply not needed. The conferences relied on donations from their local parishes' Sunday or special-needs collections. The slowly developing functions, such as special works and retail thrift stores, were operated with as small a staff as possible for many years. During the presidencies of Joe Connors (1968–1974) and Mort Staub (1974–1980), however, it became clear that more financial planning was needed. Jim Gallagher, a CPA with a master's degree from Harvard, served as the treasurer under Jim Finnerty and upgraded the accounting system. During these times, SVdP Phoenix was forced to borrow funds from the Phoenix Diocese on numerous occasions. By the early 1990s, Brian O'Donnell, the treasurer, began to provide detailed financial reports at each board meeting. With the expansion of 420 West Watkins Road in the 1990s, many operations were consolidated and administrative personnel was added.

According to Terry Wilson, SVdP Phoenix was actually insolvent when he came into office. The charity dining hall on Ninth Street was "atrociously bad." But the early problems were overcome, and there ensued a long period of construction until the mid-1990s. Wilson remembered that the money didn't really start coming in until after a statue of St. Joseph was buried at 420 West Watkins Road. On a more mundane level, financial recovery came when Wilson suggested that 10 percent of all bequests go into board-restricted funds as a cash reserve. "That really helped during the recession," he said. Wilson also established an executive committee made up of officers from the board of directors. Today, the executive committee establishes the agenda and provides information in advance of board meetings in order to be prepared. Wilson set up a rule that said members of the executive committee must attend a district meeting at least once a month.

Ronald Meyer had started establishing bylaws to bring organization to the society, and Terry Wilson continued the process. Meyer set up the legal component, and Wilson set up the processes. The board was composed of six Vincentians and six people appointed by the president; the president was a Vincentian and would break any ties, so the Vincentians would always have a majority. "How did we become so successful?" Meyer asked. "We were open to other people and exchanged ideas freely. In those days, when I became president, there were no mandatory classes on how to become a Vincentian. We now have the best education in the country. You need training. Always make home visits with two people—always."

During this period of accomplishments, the society's sister council in Cuernavaca was also expanding at a fantastic rate. In 1992, inspired by a visit to the former dining room on Ninth Avenue and Madison Street, two members returned to Cuernavaca and began a feeding program at the San Juan Evangelista Church. Each Saturday, food was prepared in homes and served on benches in the church garden for families in the area. A few years later, in 1998, SVdP Cuernavaca obtained land provided by the State of Morelos and continued serving breakfast on Saturdays. Many local restaurants and bakeries began to provide food for the meals, and the program slowly expanded. The program was also initiated in a barrio called Jardin Juarez, where it continued until 2017.

Matt Scott and Dan O'Meara led the April 1996 celebratory parade, which started at St. Mary's Basilica, SVdP Phoenix's first location.

In 1996, SVdP Phoenix celebrated its fiftieth anniversary. At that time, there were seventy-eight parish conferences, three special works conferences and four additional ministries. The organization numbered over two thousand members. It remained profoundly spiritual. Conference meetings began with opening prayers, followed by a spiritual reading and discussion and closed with prayers. The fiftieth-anniversary celebration started on Sunday, April 28, 1996. The celebration began with a mass of thanksgiving, which was attended by nine hundred guests and held at SVdP Phoenix's birthplace, St. Mary's Basilica. Bishop Thomas J. O'Brien and Reverend Warren Rouse, OFM, offered praise for reaching this historic milestone. Immediately after the celebration, two of the Phoenix founding fathers, Matt Scott and Dan O'Meara, led a grand and triumphant procession from St. Mary's Basilica to the Hyatt Regency Hotel for a celebratory reception. The keynote speaker was Sister Mary Rose McGeady, who encouraged all in attendance to continuously look around to meet the needs of the poor and thus carry out SVdP Phoenix's mission. A booklet documenting SVdP Phoenix's history from 1946 to 1996 was published; a similar booklet was published ten years later to document the society's sixty-year history.

In 1992, it was clear that the Ninth Avenue and Madison Street site was no longer adequate, and it would have been costly to repair. At that time, clinic services consisted mainly of dental extractions and dentures for people contracted through Phoenix's Healthcare for the Homeless. Medical services were sporadic and limited. Cathy Cordova, who was then the clinic administrator, dreamed of a new clinic, where medical, dental and social services could be integrated. The unfinished space at 420 West Watkins Road was intended to replace the services at the Madison site; however, healthcare was in limbo due to its complexity and expense. A decision needed to be made on whether to close the clinic entirely or put forth a major new effort.

A historical booklet published in 1996 for SVdP Phoenix's fifty-year celebration; in 2006, a similar booklet was published to mark the sixtieth anniversary.

Earl J. Baker, MD, fortuitously arrived on the scene. He was well known in the community for pioneering the first open-heart surgery in Phoenix. On retiring,

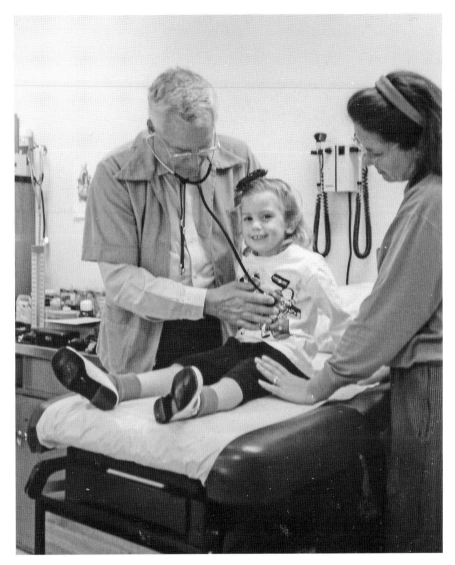

Dr. Earl J. Baker, who directed the SVdP Phoenix medical and dental clinic for many years, with young patient.

the Maricopa Medical Society sent him on a mission to start a free clinic in south Phoenix for the uninsured working poor. SVdP Phoenix allowed Dr. Baker to pursue the prospect of a new and expanded medical and dental clinic; making sure the clinic was not a financial burden was a major concern. In Dr. Baker's pursuit of funding, he would later chuckle that Maricopa Medical Center (now Maricopa Integrated Health) could not help him with money but would "lend him a couple of master's in healthcare administration interns." "What help could they be?" he thought. Little did he know that they were two very experienced and passionate healthcare leaders who would prove to be instrumental in the realization and transformation of a new clinic. Ann Rea had experience as a hospital laboratory medical technologist, and Janice Ertl was an experienced registered nurse in critical care and risk management. They took over the conflicted fundraising and facility design committees, respectively, and made progress so that the entire second floor of the Watkins building was dedicated for a clinic that opened in March 1994.

Ertl stayed with SVdP Phoenix and became the clinic administrator and later director. "When Dr. Baker came along, we raised our own money and brought in our own new set of donors," she said. "We enlisted hospitals and healthcare companies to provide services for our patients. We relied heavily on volunteers but needed some staff structure so that volunteers could come in, feel that they were accomplishing care and leave trusting that staff would follow through. They generally committed to four hours a month." Ertl also believed that they had to win the trust of the clients, many of whom distrusted anyone who asked them questions because they were not in the country legally. Payton Cooper painted a beautiful mural in the original Watkins Clinic that featured St. Vincent de Paul, Blessed Frederic Ozanam and numerous animals and children gathered around a pool, where they saw reflections of themselves as made whole. "Our reputation as a safe place spread rapidly. We got to the point where we could ask very sensitive questions and [clients] would answer without hesitation."

Services were expanded from a "band-aid" approach to a more holistic approach. Dental services were a prime example of this. The philosophy changed from providing emergency extractions to completing restorations that made the mouth pain-free and aesthetically pleasing. This often meant a year or longer commitment on the part of the adult patient due to the severity of disease.

The staff did not consider the clinic as a static operation. "We exploited any opportunities," said Ertl. "I always saw things as evolving. You must keep your eyes open to the needs of the community and be ready to respond." Children's dental was a huge need for the many children who did not qualify for the Arizona Health Care Cost Containment System (AHCCCS, Arizona's Medicaid). Dental care was also very expensive, and children were a special population. Conversely, school-based health clinics were opening, they had funding and they wanted dental care for their kids. "It was a perfect

A wall mural created by and painted in the clinic by Payton Cooper, featuring Frederic Ozanam surrounded by animals and children beside healing waters.

In 1996, Dr. Ken Snyder joined SVdP Phoenix as the director of the dental clinic.

opportunity for us," said Ertl. "Dr. Ken Snyder came on in 1996 as the children's dentist. It was a win-win. We were getting paid to provide a service for a need that we desperately wanted to fill, and Phoenix Memorial and Phoenix Baptist Hospitals paid us to provide dentistry for their school-based healthcare clinics." The clinic also expanded its focus from disease treatment to prevention and management. Dental hygiene services were an integral component of dental services from the beginning. The Family Diabetes Program began in 2000, at a time when there were few resources in Arizona that could assist Spanish-speaking clients in managing their chronic diseases.

A significant factor that helped the medical and dental clinic evolve its services was the upsurge in local philanthropy. Not-for-profit hospitals were being sold and turned into for-profit entities. The sale of these community assets would become healthcare foundations. Private philanthropists such as Virginia G. Piper would leave a legacy that targeted healthcare. All would be eager to make signature grants. "We were already a reputable clinic and had established relationships with the philanthropists, so we were a natural to receive this initial funding," Ertl said. The clinic found it possible to retain its independence while following the ideals of SVdP Phoenix. "We wanted conscientiously to follow the mission of St. Vincent de Paul. We wanted to establish trust with the board of directors," said Ertl. "We also wanted to provide high-quality healthcare. We always got what we needed. There was a lot of searching, but we knew all of the avenues out there."

Under Ertl, the clinic grew to serve sixteen thousand visits a year, roughly split in half between medical and dental visits. There were 160 regular medical and dental volunteers as well as students and residents. Multiple specialty services were offered for both medical and dental patients. Services were provided on site and at outreach children's dental clinics. Ertl retired at the end of 2015. Dr. Maurice Lee followed her as medical director, and Dr. Ken Snyder continued as dental director.

Dr. John L. Friedman wrote in the late 1090s:

> *I've been working at the St. Vincent de Paul Free Medical and Dental Clinic since the day it opened at its new facility on West Watkins in March 1994. I've been here eighty-one times so far, providing medical care for a large group of Americans who do not have health insurance, cannot afford to go to a physician or even buy prescription medications.*

After talking about what good patients they generally were, he continued with a description of their illnesses:

Most of what I see in the clinic is chronic illness: asthma, obstructive pulmonary disease, tuberculosis, diabetes, morbid obesity, arthritis, chronic anxiety and depression and chronic dental diseases. Most of the medicines for asthma, COPD, arthritis and depression are so expensive that my patients cannot begin to afford to fill their prescriptions. We have a large number and variety of medicines donated to the clinic free of charge. But sometimes, we don't have what the patient needs. Genrich Pharmacy on East Virginia Avenue in Phoenix provides prescription medications with very little mark up, enabling our patients the opportunity to obtain medication which they would not have otherwise.

This is the stark reality of the clinic. Despite legislative efforts put forward throughout the years to alleviate the need for affordable healthcare in America, enactments are often offset with freezes and exclusions. There will always be individuals and needs left out; there will always be a role for a charity clinic.

On April 16, 1994, the medical and dental clinic held a fundraising dinner at the Scottsdale Pavilion. Celebrity roasts were popular on television at that time. Following this model, the "victim" of the celebrity roast was Pulitzer Prize–winning political cartoonist Steve Benson. The dinner included many

On April 16, 1994, the medical and dental clinic hosted a celebrity roast to honor Steve Benson, a cartoonist for the *Arizona Republic*.

celebrities, including Barry Goldwater, Michael Grant, Jane Hull, Bob "Boze" Bell, Sam Steiger and Hugh Downs. The event raised $80,000 for the SVdP Phoenix Clinic.

Terry Wilson understood the need for a strong organized spiritual direction that could guide SVdP Phoenix into the future. The society's members agreed that, as members of a Catholic organization, they would always follow Catholic teachings but asked themselves how they may best apply their services to meet the spiritual needs of their clients and members. In 1994, President Terry Wilson asked Steve Jenkins and conference coordinator John Feit to create a spirituality committee. At that time, only few official publications were available, including the rules and manual of the society, some writings of St. Vincent de Paul and Frederic Ozanam and a few publications from the SVdP National Office in St. Louis. The national office had no designated employees charged with this responsibility, so the emphasis on spirituality fell to the individual diocesan and particular councils and conferences. Since there had been few—if any—prior gatherings of conference and district council spiritual advisors in Phoenix, a Saturday meeting was organized. About forty spiritual advisors responded, many of them priests and religious individuals. The meeting began with an extended reflection on a document of excerpts from the rules and the writings of St. Vincent de Paul and Frederic Ozanam. During the reflection, practically all of the attendees contributed comments and suggestions, and it was agreed by all that such a format could generate fruitful dialogue and ideas for further reflections. This was the beginning of the spiritual advisor workshops.

It was also apparent that many of the priests and deacons were hard-pressed to attend conference meetings regularly and that little information on the spirituality of St. Vincent de Paul and the writings of Frederic Ozanam was readily available to spiritual advisors. Central coordination was needed to develop materials and to begin to educate and train individual conference members to be spiritual advisors. In addition, little was known about which conferences had permanent regular spiritual advisors. As a result, the spirituality committee began to address the conferences' concerns, and they began to take opportunities to promote Vincentian spirituality and reflection in conference meetings. The spirituality committee, a subcommittee of the conference concerns committee, began meeting monthly. Initially, the committee developed goals and a set of objectives: to survey the conferences to determine if there were active spiritual advisors; to establish annual days of reflection for conference members; to establish a format for a workshop for conference spiritual advisors and provide the workshops on a timely basis; and to develop a set of resources to assist conference spiritual advisors.

The survey of conferences revealed that many of them did not have permanent spiritual advisors, and many were not using the spiritual reflection time during conference meetings. A major goal of the spirituality committee was to have an active spiritual advisor in each conference and district of SVdP Phoenix. This was achieved through the spiritual advisor workshops, which trained lay spiritual advisors, members who were invited by the president of each conference. To stress the importance of the spiritual advisor in the conference, spiritual advisor workshops were structured for both the spiritual advisor and the president of the conference or district council. These workshops were held every six months at the Dan O'Meara Center and also on request for conferences in outlying districts.

The first day of reflection was held at St. Theresa Catholic Church in Phoenix and was conducted by national episcopal advisor Lawrence J. McNamara, the Bishop of the Diocese of Grand Island, Nebraska. It was well attended. Subsequent days of reflection were held, but in time, the event was changed to a half day of reflection, usually beginning with mass and followed by a morning event.

By 2000, the spirituality committee was augmented by three conference coordinators, John Feit, Michael Syslo and Jerry Castro. The chairperson, Father Tom Bielawa, SDS (Society of the Divine Savior), was the pastor of St. William Church in Cashion, Arizona, and he was also the spiritual advisor for District Eight in the southwest part of the valley. Other members included then-president Nancy Spencer; Steve Jenkins; Bill Ringer, president of District Six; Sister Lawrence Bergs, SDS; and Sister Roqueta Zappa, RSM (Religious Sisters of Mercy). Both Sister Lawrence and Sister Roqueta were very familiar with SVdP Phoenix. Sister Lawrence was one of the founders of the Ministry to the Homeless, and Sister Roqueta, a certified social worker, had been associated with special ministries for many years. The committee became very active under Father Tom, and with the help of the conference coordinator staff, it began to develop formats for the spiritual advisor workshops and the first spiritual advisor handbook. This handbook was eventually upgraded and released by the national council for use by conferences throughout the United States. By the beginning of the 2000s, almost all of the conferences had active spiritual advisors.

In 1996, Jack Ahern, a member of Our Lady of Perpetual Help Conference in Glendale, and his prayer partner, Carney Dirkson, developed a workshop titled "Praying with the People We Serve." The workshop was

A family participating in SVdP Phoenix's Adopt A Family Christmas program.

Food delivery by Bashas' to SVdP Phoenix's reclamation center. Carl Diemeke, a former food warehouse manager, is on the left; the current manager is Mary Thomas.

widely popular and focused on methods of praying with families on home visits. The practice has been widely accepted and used by conference visiting teams. Jack and his current prayer partner, Roseanne Gutierrez, are still holding the workshops. The idea has also been integrated into the Ozanam Formation Experience, which is training offered to all new members.

By the end of the 2000s, most of the goals and objectives of the original spiritual committee had been achieved. There were spiritual advisors in every conference and district, and they are now listed in the directory of conferences. Spiritual advisor workshops were ongoing, and mornings of reflection were held on a regular basis.

During this time period, the Adopt A Family Christmas program was established. Conferences would identify a struggling family and place their name on a list of families to be adopted for Christmas. The program was well-advertised, and corporations and families would contact SVdP Phoenix to recommend a family it could adopt for Christmas. The sponsor was then asked to provide the adopted family with a gift for each family member and Christmas dinner. The sponsor was also asked to personally meet and deliver the gifts to the family. The program proved to be a great success and continues to this day. It should be noted that the greatest benefit of the program is not the giving of gifts, but the personal face-to-face contact of those who can sustain themselves with those who are struggling to survive. Most find that both families are fundamentally the same, with the primary difference being economic. The adopted family also sees that those who have greater resources are decent, good individuals. Many sponsors and adopted families come away with new perspectives of each other.

During this period of major accomplishments, the food bank and warehouse facilities also expanded. An additional fifteen-thousand-square-foot dry area was added, as well as a twenty-thousand-cubic-foot drive-in perishable cooler. Carl Diemeke was hired to manage the food bank. In 1996, the reclamation tonnage had increased from an initial start of one million pounds annually to more than five million pounds annually. During this period, the food bank provided food to more than sixty conferences, necessitating the development of food pantry guidelines. The methodology of creating monthly food allotments, pickup and delivery schedules and time frames was also put in place and continues to this day.

5

LOOKING TO THE FUTURE

1996 to 2014

During the eighteen-year period between 1996 and 2014, three elected presidents served: Nancy Spencer, Steve Jenkins and Joe Riley. Nancy Spencer was the first woman to serve as the president of St. Vincent de Paul Phoenix. A retired director of nursing, Spencer became president on October 1, 1996. Steve Zabilski was hired as the executive director a month later. Spencer was present forty hours a week and was a hands-on visionary. The organization continued to grow, both in spirituality and in the number of people building a relationship with the community. During the time that Spencer was president, the chapel was built, and the statue of Frederic Ozanam was erected. Spencer also started the Top Hat Award, which was given to people who had conspicuously aided SVdP Phoenix. As the name indicated, the award contained a raised image of a top hat. Frederic Ozanam wore a top hat, and this special award was meant to signify a gracious SVdP Phoenix appreciation of the person who received the award. In the past, the award has been given to individuals who have made a special contribution to the advancement of the society's mission. Early pioneer founders have received this award, as have influential individuals, such as Rabbi Albert Plotkin, Governor Rose Mofford, Norm McClelland and Eddie Basha. The award is now only given intermittently. Nancy Spencer died in 2005 at the age of sixty-eight.

Steve Zabilski remembered, "There was a strong desire to grow the society, more people working to serve the poor, expanded services to help even more people in new ways, more businesses involved. We acquired additional property around 420 West Watkins and anticipated future growth."

Top Hat Award recipients Matt Scott, Dan O'Meara, Mickey McBinn and Henry Unger.

The year 2001 was an active one for the society; with the purchase of the Sunnyslope thrift store property, SVdP Phoenix owned five thrift stores. New showers were built for special ministry clients. The One at a Time scholarship program began assisting high school graduates who were the first in their families to attend college. In 2002, SVdP Phoenix provided financial assistance and resources to aid firefighting efforts, working in conjunction with the Red Cross, Salvation Army and the Payson Conference in fighting the Rodeo Chediski Forest Fire. The Biblical Prayer Garden was dedicated by Peter Maland in honor of his wife, Sadie; it was financed through the sale of one-hundred-dollar engraved bricks. Students from Brophy College Preparatory also contributed their time and talent to the Biblical Garden.

A sad milestone was met when Matt Scott died in January 2004. Scott, the last of the early founders, was still serving SVdP Phoenix when he died at age ninety-seven; he told stories of the society's early days to fill in the gaps of its history. The *Vincentian* wrote:

> *Over a fifty-year period, Scott maintained an abiding interest in the Society of St. Vincent de Paul…but he refused to micromanage from the sidelines.…He would venture an opinion if requested, but never second guessed a decision made and ratified by the society's ruling body. Well*

into his 90s, he and his wife, Glennie, could be found side by side, sorting
donated clothing in the society's processing center on Watkins Road.

Scott's best-remembered summary of the early years was: "We did what we had to do with what we had at hand, and we had a good time doing it."

More happily, in 2004, SVdP Phoenix observed its Thirty-Millionth Meal Celebration on March 3 to honor its continuous meal service since 1954. The *Vincentian Connection* magazine observed that not a day had been missed since the first meal was served in 1954 and that five dining rooms were operating, preparing more than three thousand meals each day in its kitchen on Watkins Road.

During Spencer's presidency, the Human Services Campus (HSC) was developed, and initial functions continued under President Steve Jenkins. The dining room on Ninth Avenue was outdated, and for several years, the area surrounding the dining room on Madison Avenue in downtown Phoenix had experienced a dramatic increase in the number of people it served. This was partially the result of a growing city and other changes to the downtown business center that was within blocks of the dining room. SVdP Phoenix representatives joined a coalition of other providers to the homeless community and petitioned the city and Maricopa County to build the HSC. Maricopa County supervisors Mary Rose Wilcox, Andy Kunasek, Fulton Brock, Don Stapley and Jan Brewer and county manager David Smith decided to build an entire HSC, incorporating services like SVdP Phoenix, Central Arizona Shelter Services (CASS), St. Joseph the Worker, Nova Safe Haven, Lodestar Day Resource Center and the Maricopa County Health Clinic. The idea of the campus was to concentrate as many agencies as possible to enable the poor to get direct access to help. As a result, Maricopa County purchased property near the dining room with the intent to provide comprehensive services to people living primarily on the streets.

In January 2003, the board of SVdP Phoenix approved a resolution about becoming a member, and it agreed to certain legal responsibilities that would also be required from each of the member organizations. Once signed, the Operating Agreement of Human Services Campus, LLC. Maricopa County became the legal mechanism that allowed for the construction of the buildings in the area that would serve participating agencies. This agreement ultimately led SVdP Phoenix to become an owner of the SVdP feeding center, a part of the HSC that opened in 2005.

The new SVdP Phoenix Henry Unger Dining Room was completed and dedicated on November 16, 2005. This new dining room initially served the noon meal seven days a week. On April 3, 2006, the dining room also began serving breakfast Monday through Friday. When the Henry Unger Dining Room began serving breakfast, employees of companies in the area began to volunteer on a regular basis. Teams from these companies volunteered, and the idea spread throughout the Phoenix area. Thus began a program of corporate partners that has grown to over four hundred companies that provide volunteers to the many ministries of SVdP Phoenix today.

In the end, this collaboration built one of the finest human services centers in the entire country. It is truly like a college campus, in that numerous services are all combined—food, clothing, counseling, shelter and medical care in one spot—which is very important to those living on the streets. To this day, it remains one of the society's signature accomplishments.

When SVdP Phoenix was given land for its dining area, it also received a deed to land that included an extra parcel of about one-third of an acre to the east of the dining room to allow for future expansion. No plans were contemplated for years, until a citizens committee was formed to explore the possibility of converting this vacant land into a garden. Cathy Eden, a local professor of public administration at Arizona State

Blessing of the garden adjacent to SVdP Phoenix's dining room at the HSC by Father Emile "Bud" Pelletier, then SVdP Phoenix's spiritual advisor.

University, chaired the committee. The charge of the committee was to see if SVdP Phoenix was willing to allow a community-type garden to be planted on the site to grow food for the dining room. In addition, clients and volunteers would be able to experience uplifting and therapeutic time working in and enjoying the garden.

The citizens committee brought different skills and resources to the project. It accomplished the task of clearing the land of broken glass, asphalt, concrete and debris. Garden planners brought in riverwash soil to raise the bed about ten inches above grade in order to not disturb any Native American artifacts beneath the soil. Finally, another four to five inches of compost from Singh Farms was applied to begin converting the inert soil to healthy organic loam. Shade trees were donated, as was an irrigation system. The garden was ready for use. Vegetable and fruit tree growing was started in 2012, with the citizens committee encouraging the widest possible participation from the community. Volunteers did show up and kept adding and adapting resources to make the garden work. The garden grew in land under cultivation and in the number of people involved. Local community garden activists found the garden to be a safe and enjoyable place to work and play. A steady supply of food made its way next door to the dining room for salads, side dishes and meal garnishes.

In 2005, the original Henry Unger Dining Room closed after fifty-one years of serving the poor. Temple Beth Israel's rabbi, Robert Plotkin, who had been serving Christmas and Easter meals since 1960, gave the invocation at the closing ceremony. The new Henry Unger Memorial Dining Room at the new HSC opened immediately thereafter. Meanwhile, the Turkey Tuesday program with Bashas' grocery stores reached a record twenty thousand turkeys donated to SVdP Phoenix. Channel 12 KPNX-TV and KMLE Country 107.9 FM provided media coverage.

In that same year, Dan Heiple helped lead many volunteers, including several members of the Order of Malta, like Jeanne O'Brien, Steve Zabilski, Ray Daoust and Joe Riley, in serving at Ozanam Manor. The Order of Malta originated during the Crusades as an effort to protect the Holy Land. Today, the knights' and dames' mission has changed to combatting poverty. The order made Ozanam Manor one of its signature projects in Phoenix, aiding in providing financial support and hosting special events. The Order of Malta is an actual order of the Catholic Church and is formally seated at the United Nations.

The medical and dental clinics began holding a fundraising breakfast in 2005, and Ozanam Manor followed suit in 2006, bringing in some $100,000.

Turkeys donated by shoppers at local grocery stores on Turkey Tuesday, along with a food box, are distributed to families to enjoy a Thanksgiving meal.

Now, one fundraising breakfast is held to benefit all of the programs and ministries. In 2013, a notice was received that funding would be cut because the City of Phoenix planned to demolish and redevelop the area without Ozanam Manor. No funds were available to move the residents from the 1730 East Monroe Street property into another facility. SVdP Phoenix's board of directors agreed to rebuild the facility on a Watkins Road property but stipulated that the cash must be raised in advance. This led to the highly successful Building a Resilient Community capital campaign. Steve Attwood, the current president of SVdP Phoenix, noted that the capital campaign raised $15 million from donors, in addition to the normal operating revenues required each year. "The successful drive spoke to the reputation of St. Vincent de Paul," he said. "People love our mission, continuity of business in the community, our leadership and our reputation. Our name in this community is gold."

Ozanam Manor was only one reason for the capital campaign. The board of SVdP Phoenix envisioned an expanded facility, much like the HSC, providing a wide range of services for the poor. With what had become its normal attitude of championing the cause of the poor, the campaign also advanced "the significant expansion of [the society's] medical and dental clinics by remodeling existing space" and an "enhanced urban farm to expand sustainable nutrient-dense food resources for those [the society] serves, create opportunities for additional partnerships, and serve as a teaching and research development site in [the society's] community," along with numerous other goals. It marked the final evolution of the West Watkins Road property into a sort of nucleus of the SVdP Phoenix enterprise, and it marked tremendous growth from a meeting of five men in 1946 at St. Mary's Rectory scrabbling for whatever resources they could find.

SVdP Phoenix had firmly established itself on Watkins Road in South Phoenix and extended its reach throughout much of central and northern Arizona. Steve Jenkins became president in 2003. He strongly supported more education for the Vincentian membership. At the December 2002 board meeting, Tom Clouser, chairperson of the conference resources and concerns committee, presented the formation and training proposal. This proposal established a comprehensive training program for all the members of SVdP Phoenix. The training program was a product of the formation subcommittee led by chairperson and Arizona State University professor Hal White. The program consisted of training modules and was named the Ozanam Formation Experience (OFE). This new OFE replaced the traditional Ozanam School that had been in place since SVdP Phoenix began in Arizona. The OFE consisted of four three-hour segments that dealt with the history, spirituality, home visits, structure and operation of SVdP Phoenix and its conferences. "The challenge was that, as the society had grown larger, many new members did not know the history or the rules," said White.

It is important to credit Vincentian Support Services (VSS) for its efforts on behalf of these new requirements. During 2002, it was recognized that trying to pass any resolution requiring or obligating members to attend special training was not going to pass unless the members were convinced that the new rules were important and needed to be passed. For most of the year, VSS staff visited conferences and promoted the need for this special training. During this period, VSS expanded, hiring staff members Patricia Metrick and Jerry Castro, so it was important that they be trained as quickly as possible. Both fit well with what needed to be accomplished.

After a vote was taken by the SVdP Phoenix board to move ahead, presentations of the program were given to districts and conferences. This proposal was controversial and required extensive discussions at two general membership meetings before it was brought to a final vote for adoption at a third general membership meeting held in September 2003, nine months after the original proposal was approved by the board and forwarded to the membership. The OFE became mandatory for all new members, with existing members being exempt from the requirement or "grandfathered." New members who completed the OFE became enhanced members and were initiated with a special blessing along with a medal immediately after mass at each general membership meeting. As the program progressed, many of the old members and all of the new members received this training. As a result, members who completed the OFE shared a common knowledge of SVdP Phoenix, based on its rules, history, spirituality and local practices.

However, in the years after the introduction of OFE training began, it became evident that many longtime members who had been "grandfathered" and had become officers needed to be updated on the new rules of the society and other changes in order to be effective leaders. In 2006, the SVdP Phoenix Board passed an additional resolution that required OFE completion for all officers at all levels—council, district and conference. When presented with the resolution, the general membership approved it; since then, all officers have been OFE-certified.

With OFE training being required many times during the year in various locations within SVdP Phoenix, VSS was very busy providing training as well as other services. For a period of time, VSS maintained a call-in line for assistance. Volunteers staffed the phones and forwarded calls for help to various conferences. During this period of time, Sandy Edwards became a valued member of the staff. In 2009, Mike Syslo resigned and took the position of associate director at the national office in St. Louis; Patricia Metrick became the head of Vincentian Support Services. Today, John Junker serves as the director of this important department, which has greatly expanded the services it provides to Vincentians throughout Arizona.

In 2016, a class to supplement OFE called Ozanam Rejuvenation was developed by the spirituality and formation committee. It was used to update members on changes that occurred in the years following their introduction through OFE. Presently, OFE and Ozanam Rejuvenation serve to not only educate new members but to provide continuing education to all members.

Throughout the life of SVdP Phoenix, respect and assistance have been earned from many individuals, some from other religions and others who were well-known in the community. This support continues to provide visibility, credibility and recognition. Who provided the society with the resources it needed to continue to serve the poor? In the early years, it was people like

Businessman Jimmy Walker's Never Give Up Program brings prominent individuals to share a message of hope and encouragement weekly at the Henry Unger Dining Room.

Rabbi Albert Plotkin and Joe Garagiola who provided this assistance. For several years, Mary Jo West, who had been a very popular television reporter with **KPNX** Channel 12, was a member of the society's staff.

In 2006, the Henry Unger Dining Room began hosting Bible studies in an all-purpose room led by Phoenix businessman Jimmy Walker. During the Monday morning sessions, Walker introduced people to the society's guests, who shared challenges in their lives and how they turned to God and others for help. Later that year, Walker expanded the program into the main dining room and installed a state-of-the-art sound and closed-circuit television system so that everyone attending breakfast could hear and see the invited guests. The program, Never Give Up, offered hope to the guests of changing their lives through the examples of the invited speakers. The first Never Give Up speaker was Bob Lanier, an NBA Hall of Fame basketball star. To provide an additional incentive for the guests eating breakfast to stay in the room and listen to the speaker, Bob Russell, a former member of the board of directors and longtime SVdP Phoenix supporter, provided ten-dollar McDonald's gift cards, which were raffled at the end of each talk.

This program has been very successful and has motivated many to turn their lives around. It has also provided the major benefit of bringing local and national leaders and people who are experiencing homelessness together to share their stories from their hearts. Some of the speakers Walker has introduced through the years have included Jerry Colangelo, the former owner of the Phoenix Suns; Harvey Mackay, a syndicated columnist and writer; Larry Fitzgerald, an Arizona Cardinals wide receiver; Andrea Bocelli, an Italian opera singer; and Muhammad and Lonnie Ali. Steve Zabilski remembered that Muhammad Ali loved to visit the society's dining rooms, where he enjoyed serving the society's guests. Another instantly recognizable sports figure who often visited was Meadowlark Lemon, who shot baskets with the society's guests. "He was an inspiring man," said Zabilski. "I don't think I ever saw him without a Bible in his hand." Never Give Up continues to this day, thanks to the efforts of Walker. Hundreds of different speakers, including the author of this book, have presented messages of hope to the society's dining room guests.

Stephen Jenkins presided over the revision of SVdP Phoenix's bylaws; they were to conform to national standards, its growth in number of conferences and to the number and independence of committees. In 2007, in order to conform the bylaws to the Council of the United States' model bylaws, a bylaws committee was created. The existing bylaws had been in effect since 1987 and needed to be reformatted and brought up to date based on the national model. After months of study and revision, the proposed bylaws were approved by the SVdP Phoenix board and referred to the districts and conferences for review and, if necessary, modification. After review and discussion at the December 2007 and March 2008 general membership meetings, the bylaws were approved at the June 14, 2008 general membership meeting. The bylaws that governed the districts and conferences were later developed by the bylaws committee and ultimately approved at subsequent general membership meetings.

In 2006, SVdP Phoenix celebrated its sixtieth anniversary. There were then eighty-five parish conferences and a myriad of new services; the organization numbered over five thousand members. It remained profoundly spiritual. SVdP Phoenix published a small booklet to document its history from 1946 to 2006.

Joe Riley was the president from 2008 to 2014. Riley recognized that SVdP Phoenix needed to raise its revenue significantly and "strengthen its financial foundation." His top priority was "to expand the scope and enhance the sophistication of [the society's] development (fundraising) efforts to secure the resources needed." In other words, what he planned was not a series of lurches but a continuing flow forward, supported on firm foundations.

Cardinal great Larry Fitzgerald comforting a homeless woman.

Steve Zabilski, Mohammed Ali and Nancy Spencer surrounded by children at the Dan O'Meara Center, located at 420 West Watkins Street, Phoenix, Arizona.

Community-based fundraising and activities became commonplace. The Virginia G. Piper Charitable Trust has provided millions of dollars in support over the past nineteen years. But at this pivotal time, a grant was secured from the Piper Trust to specifically focus on allowing SVdP Phoenix to expand and build its fundraising and development efforts. The grant provided the resources that enabled the creation of programs that aided fundraising. "We updated our website, expanded special events, improved our advertising and outreach and generally raised money for programs we otherwise would not have. It took us from good to great, really elevated us to another level, making St. Vincent de Paul a major player," noted Zabilski. Riley remains proud of SVdP Phoenix's relationship with the Piper Trust, which resulted in the creation of the Piper and Pallotta Project and a productive partnership with Advertising for Humanity. A key component of the project was the addition of several new staff positions, one of which was a major gift officer. The focus on fundraising resulted in donor transactions and contributions rising in each of the six years of his presidency. "The success of this bold initiative can best be measured by a substantial boost in revenue and a very strong financial position, the outstanding performance of our development and marketing staffs and unprecedented community support," he said. Riley believes Phoenix has the finest development team of any SVdP Council in the United States.

In 2013, the board created an advisory council to help guide development efforts with the purpose of bringing together community leaders to advise staff. Craig Weatherup, a former chairman and CEO of Pepsi-Cola, agreed to lead the effort. He invited local philanthropists and other community leaders to offer their counsel and support to SVdP Phoenix. The advisory council has been an extremely valuable asset for the society's fundraising efforts.

When Riley was first elected, the thrift stores were financial drains. In 2008, SVdP Phoenix responded with its Save Our Stores campaign, which was later called Serve Our Stores. After several years, the thrift stores' profitability improved. This was accomplished through better management, innovative programs and increased support from the conferences. The Serve Our Stores committee was created to support the operation of the thrift stores, and it continues to do so.

The Catholic Diocese of Phoenix, responding to the need for training to protect potential victims from sexual abuse, implemented the Called to Protect abuse prevention program. Certification through this program was required of all volunteers involved in parish ministries, including members of SVdP Phoenix. This policy remains in place today.

In 2011, the Hall of Banners at the Dan O'Meara Center, which was, in many ways, a signature part of SVdP Phoenix, was remodeled in conjunction with the City of Phoenix. The Phoenix Aviation Department funded the $1.2-million effort as part of a noise-abatement program related to Phoenix Sky Harbor International Airport. The noise created by planes flying overhead was lessened; the building gained an improved sound system, better air circulation and temperature control; and both utility and maintenance costs were reduced. All agreed that the new Hall of Banners was much nicer than the old one. It was a great transformation of the facility.

Also in 2011, at Riley's invitation, Michael Thio, St. Vincent de Paul's international president general, attended the Western Regional Meeting, which was hosted by SVdP Phoenix. President Thio lived in Singapore; Phoenix was his only stop in the United States, a true honor for the society's regional conference.

In 2012, Riley enlisted the expertise of past president Terry Wilson, and a dedicated committee created the first strategic plan for the organization, which produced such meaningful initiatives as the Ozanam Rejuvenation Program and bilingual OFE training. Recognizing the key role of youth, the annunciation Catholic school Vibrant Vinnies was formed; it was an elementary conference from St. Gabriel Parish composed of members who were in grades five through eight. They supported the receiving end of food lines, sponsored an annual Christmas party, coordinated clothing drives for St. Vincent de Paul thrift stores, visited residents at Ozanam Manor and helped with Friday Pizza Night at the Dan O'Meara Center. Today, they represent SVdP Phoenix's future. The strategic plan also established a governance committee and committed St. Vincent de Paul to using new technologies and initiating new efforts to spread the good news of SVdP Phoenix.

The Human Services Campus continued to grow during Riley's term of office. It has since become a national model for its collaboration of sixteen nonprofit organizations with the shared objective of helping men and women end their homelessness. Riley acknowledged that homelessness remains a formidable challenge but noted that the agency partners are fully committed to their common goal.

The Dream Center was created in 2011 to provide children attending the Family Evening Meal at the Dan O'Meara Center the opportunity to express themselves and have an outlet for their energy. It later evolved into an after-school enrichment program during which the children have the opportunity to receive individual homework assistance; play chess and educational games; participate in experiments and other science, technology,

A family spending time in the Dream Center during the family evening meal served at the Dan O'Meara Center, Phoenix, Arizona.

engineering, arts and mathematics (STEAM) projects; read with volunteers; attend Girl Scout meetings; participate in field trips; listen to guest speakers; and receive information and guidance for college. The Dream Center also provides educational summer programs and holiday events.

Children ages four to seventeen can also participate in the activities provided at the Dream Center, which are available Monday through Friday from 4:30 to 6:00 p.m. The main objective of the center is to nurture the children's minds and spirits. Through established programs, children receive the assistance they need, with the help of staff and volunteers, to be successful in school and beyond. The Dream Center has established educational pillars that are touched on a daily, weekly or monthly basis to ensure each child is exposed to different avenues of education. The pillars are math, literacy, life skills, college access and career readiness, and they are summarized under the title of STEAM. Monday through Thursday evenings, the Dream Center's programs are broken into the following forty-five-minute blocks:

4:30–5:15 p.m.: Homework help for the first forty-five-minute block. If a child does not have homework, a homework packet by grade and twenty minutes of reading is completed with the help of a volunteer.

5:15–6:00 p.m.: The second forty-five-minute block is interactive programming. A volunteer runs an activity that focuses on one of the educational pillars. Additionally, educational games and learning tools for all ages are available for children to choose from.

6:00 p.m.: Cleanup. All Dream Center children will work alongside volunteers to help put away all activities and clean up the Dream Center at the end of the evening.

Fridays are referred to as Family Fun Days and are also scheduled from 4:30 to 6:00 p.m. Adults and children of all ages are invited to engage in various activities and special programming.

During the summer months, the Dream Center engages children in learning activities that help them to become better prepared for their next grade level. The summer programs run Monday through Thursday evenings from 4:00 to 6:00 p.m. On arrival, children check out a folder and complete bridge book materials based on grade level. There is then focused time from 4:00 to 5:15 p.m., during which children can work side by side with volunteers to complete their work. After completion, children participate in different educational activities for the remainder of the session. The children's progress is tracked throughout the summer, and each child participates in an end-of-summer rewards program and celebration. Five events are held in the Dream Center throughout the summer that celebrate learning and literacy. At the end of each event, every child receives brand-new books to take home, building their own personal libraries.

Although the society's central programs of assistance continue to provide successful benefits to its assistance of the poor, it is important to acknowledge the daily work of the conferences, whose members continue to meet face to face with those in need, providing direct assistance and financial support. There are many stories of the ways individual members of conferences have made differences to the society. One such story is that of Stane Cruce.

For the most part, conferences were funded by parish collections, twinning assistance and, when needed, financial assistance from their districts. Occasionally, a financial gift is given directly to a conference. One of the largest conference estate gifts was received in 2008; the St. Gregory Conference, one of the original conferences with an aggregation date of 1951, received a $500,000 gift from the Stane Cruce estate. Stane Cruce appeared at a St. Gregory Conference meeting in May 1996 and asked if she could become a member of the conference. She was a member of the Orthodox Church and had just returned from a trip to visit relatives in

Croatia. While in Croatia, she decided to visit Medjugorje, which turned out to be a major turning point in her life. She relayed the story of her visit by describing a spiritual encounter. Her narration was very moving, and all present were deeply affected. Cruce wanted to join the conference because she wanted to serve the poor and to become a Roman Catholic.

Cruce joined the conference and began taking calls from families who requested assistance from the St. Gregory Conference pantry on Friday mornings. She did not feel that she could do home visits. She preferred assisting with phone calls because she was retired from Mountain Bell, where she had worked as a telephone operator. She had a special concern for people who were seeking rental assistance, and she often offered to help families from her own funds. She took Rite of Christian Initiation of Adults instruction and became a Roman Catholic and a member of St. Gregory Parish. Cruce continued answering calls on Fridays for many years until she became disabled and moved to an assisted-living facility in Sun City with her husband. Before leaving, though, she told two of the members that she "would take care of the conference." That was in 2003. She and her husband both passed away about two years later.

On January 1, 2008, the St. Gregory Conference was notified by SVdP Phoenix's chief financial officer that the estate set up by Cruce and her husband had allocated $500,000 to the St. Vincent de Paul Food Pantry at St. Gregory Church. Needless to say, St. Gregory Conference members and SVdP Phoenix were surprised at such a wonderful gift. On consultation with the pastor of St. Gregory Parish, the president of District Six and chair of SVdP Phoenix's investment committee decided to invest the funds through the company that manages SVdP Phoenix's endowments. These funds were managed with the advice of the investment committee. It was determined that the St. Gregory Conference would withdraw funds monthly for use in assisting families. Cruce always wanted to assist families with rental crises, and her legacy has done just that by providing the St. Gregory Conference with the ability to assist over 180 families each year with partial or full rental assistance.

During this period, the society's sister council in Cuernavaca continued to progress and expand its services in Mexico. By 2012, Cuernavaca was known throughout Mexico; donations and volunteers were increasing, as well as requests for services. Gina Ocampo, an engineer who had been a Vincentian for eighteen years, was hired as the administrative director.

In the fall of 2004, SVdP Cuernavaca faced a new set of challenges when the Morelos state government requested SVdP to provide food for children's lunches at a primary school in Loma Esmeralda, on the outskirts of Cuernavaca. In addition to supplying food for the children's lunches, SVdP Cuernavaca began to address the severe problem of hunger in the community by providing families with monthly food boxes. SVdP Cuernavaca recruited sponsors to provide scholarships to students whose families could not afford school supplies. Local businessmen and foundations were recruited to provide funds to repair and expand the small primary school from three rooms to six rooms for grades one through six. Currently, an additional building is under construction to provide room for school activities. SVdP Cuernavaca also developed a mobile library (Biblioteca Movil) to bring books to the area every two weeks. Before this, many of the children had never even seen a picture book.

During this period, the Voice of the Poor and governance committees were started, and they remain stable and viable committees today.

6

THE LEGACY OF TODAY

2014 to 2020

In the time between 2014 and 2020, two people have served as president of St. Vincent de Paul Phoenix. Frank Barrios, the author of this book, served as the president from 2014 to 2017; at the time of this publication, Steve Attwood serves as SVdP Phoenix's president.

Several important milestones have been accomplished in the past six years. Two major development projects were completed: the Watkins Urban Farm was dedicated on January 19, 2018, and a new, two-story, $12-million building, which provides space for expanded homeless outreach programs on the first floor and holds the new Ozanam Manor transitional housing facility on the second floor, was dedicated on May 18, 2018. Moving the outreach programs to the new building allowed for the expansion of the medical and dental clinics.

Encouraged by the success of the urban farm located at the Human Services Campus (HSC), David Smith approached Steve Zabilski and requested to expand the urban farm to the Dan O'Meara Center located at 420 West Watkins Road. Smith identified the overflow parking area just north of the campus, known as the Mayflower Property, as a potential urban farm location. Zabilski agreed, and the conversion began in the fall of 2013. The garden idea was opened to the public to encourage volunteers. In fact, volunteers came in substantial numbers and began expanding the borders of the garden in every direction. Soon, garden beds were in place from Fifth Avenue to the west and to the frontage road of I-17 in the north; compost piles expanded to the Mayflower warehouse

David Smith standing next to a giant sunflower grown in one of SVdP Phoenix's three urban farms; this one is located at the Dan O'Meara Center.

building to the east. The entire lot was filled with agricultural operations by mid-2014. The official founding date of the farm is December 2014, when the current vision for the urban farm operation took shape. Zabilski suggested to Smith that he change his assignment from chief operations officer to farm manager, and Smith agreed.

Goals were set for production, and a limited staff of one was hired. The farm at the HSC dining room was added to the overall operation. Throughout 2015, an extreme transformational effort was required to remove Bermudagrass, add irrigation, plant fruit trees and ameliorate desert soils with compost and amendments. A huge composting operation was created using landscape waste, recycled food and composted chicken manure from Hickman's Farms. Fresh compost was put down after each crop harvest. Through several harvests since 2014, the farm parcel has been raised by several inches, leaving the desert soil buried beneath. The severe alkalinity of the desert soil is now far less of a factor; soil testing at a professional lab confirms this. The total production of the two farms approached twenty thousand pounds of produce in 2016.

Success breeds success, and SVdP Phoenix members in Mesa began to look at the possibility of a Mesa urban farm. In 2015, SVdP Phoenix food service staff observed that gardening land was available on the lot at 71 West Broadway in Mesa, the location of one of the society's five dining rooms. A citizens, staff and client committee was formed to pursue the idea of a third urban farm located next to this district's dining room. It did not take long for the appointment of cochair volunteer coordinators and for them to have plants in the ground. Mary Ann Ricketts and Margot Jeaureu have led the Mesa farm initiative and its expansion to about three thousand square feet of growing space. On average, five hundred pounds of produce is harvested each month, and it is all consumed at the Mesa Dining Room. Client volunteers are critical to the success of the garden. A private company, Humetrics, is now consulting on advanced fertilizing techniques. The Mesa farm is equipped with drip irrigation, shade structures and a compost operation to assure its success throughout the year. Assistance and support of materials, plants and seeds is provided by the farm at 420 West Watkins Road. There is a great spirit and joyful experience going on there.

SVdP Phoenix now owns and operates three urban farms. The three garden spaces comprising the urban farms have nearly perfected a growing method that allows successful year-round harvesting. Clients who are poor and homeless are provided with fresh, wholesome, nutrient-dense food every day in the society's dining rooms. That is what this urban farm growing method can do. The cultivation concept is to essentially create a microclimate around each fruit and vegetable in the ground. This microclimate is created by developing rich soil using drip irrigation with filtered water, adding shade as needed and growing proven varieties that thrive at certain times of year. Mulch and wood chips are used to hold in moisture. Plants are grown end to

Vegetables growing at SVdP Phoenix's urban farm at the Dan O'Meara Center. The produce can be delivered directly to the kitchen and prepared for the guests' meals.

end: one plant finishes producing and is pulled, then the next plant is planted in the old plant's place the next day. Beehives are on site to help pollination. Natural ground cover, not Bermudagrass, is allowed to cover vacant spaces. Nature abhors a vacuum, so the soil is never bare.

In 2016, the Rob and Melani Walton Foundation awarded a $1-million grant to the Dan O'Meara Urban Farm. The special funding has allowed the physical space to be upgraded, materials to be purchased and a staff member to be hired. The purchase of equipment, including a truck and chipper shredder, has helped significantly expand the operation. A Bobcat loader was purchased with grant assistance from the Diamondbacks baseball team. The heavy equipment makes it a working farm, not just a garden. The personal interest of Rob and Melani Walton, who appear at and participate in key events around the farm, has made a huge difference in encouraging innovative practices. The Waltons' grant has stimulated other donations. In-kind donations of fertilizer, tools and farm supplies have totaled tens of thousands of dollars as well. A second major grant was awarded to the farm at the HSC in 2018. The longstanding local charitable group, Downtown Phoenix Partnership, provided resources, including cash, materials and professional labor, amounting to about $250,000 in total value. Decorative touches of murals, raised beds and sidewalks make the farm operation more fun for children, who can attend junior master gardening classes taught at the farm. These improvements significantly upgraded the output potential of this farm by 100 percent.

In 2015, an opportunity was utilized to acquire a ninety-by-thirty-foot climate-controlled hoop house from a local company. The structure was donated by a farm supporter to experiment with how hydroponics, aquaponics and in-ground growing can work together. The fish operation is run by a local LLC, with a license from SVdP Phoenix to be on site. They pay "rent" with vegetables grown on the floating grow boards, and they are all fertilized by fish effluent from one-thousand-gallon water tanks of tilapia. The operation is basically high technology growing. An additional benefit of this process is the ability to use excess fish water from the tanks as fertilizer and directly apply it to in-ground grow beds. These periodic applications stimulate noticeable new plant growth and increase harvest production. This is symbiotic growing at its best.

SVdP Phoenix is a nonprofit organization engaged in supplying nearly 4,500 meals of prepared foods daily through its five dining rooms and more than twenty other nonprofit partners. Many clients who use the dining rooms have compromised health from living on the streets; they are diabetic, overweight or undernourished. Fresh food is obviously the best choice for these clients to recover faster and more fully. A dining operation that can provide fresh, healthy food is meeting clients at the point of their needs. Food from the farms is often less than hours old when it is served. The challenge is growing the operation to a scale where it is meaningful compared to the demand. Recent months have resulted in harvests of three thousand pounds—and up to five thousand pounds in June 2019—from all three farms combined. The objective is allowing this to occur, eventually, on a year-round basis.

The members of the SVdP Phoenix board of directors and the Rob and Melani Walton Foundation are the visionaries who saw the possibilities of making this onsite farm idea work, especially by colocating farm operations with dining rooms in three locations, with the possibility of four with the recent addition of grow beds at the Sunnyslope location. The final piece of the operation was hiring serious, experienced gardeners and farmers to fill the three staff positions. All staff members have either years of growing experience across the country, special training in sustainability from Arizona State University or have come up through the ranks over the recent years, learning how to apply the SVdP Phoenix grow method.

The Dan O'Meara Center expansion opened in 2018, housing Ozanam Manor, transitional housing for older adults, and expanded facilities for outreach programs.

Volunteers are considered students at every volunteer experience. Clients are encouraged to get their hands dirty and cleanse their hurts in the process. Farm support from the society's facilities department and front office is key to keeping the farm operating efficiently. The farm takes its cost-effectiveness responsibility seriously by adding value wherever possible to further the SVdP Phoenix mission.

In 2018, the same year as the completion of the society's new facility, Ozanam Manor served 184 individuals, accounting for 17,314 bed nights. Recently, Ozanam Manor expanded its programs to include assistance to veterans by identifying those who are enrolled in Veterans Affairs Healthcare and providing these individuals with assistance. Once inside Ozanam Manor, veterans receive a safe place to live, three meals per day and assistance in finding permanent housing. A case manager assists them in identifying their barriers to housing and helps them develop a plan to address those barriers.

The director of shelter services, Mike Bell, retired in 2018 and was replaced by Julia Matthies, who is overwhelmed by the good that Ozanam Manor has done for the Phoenix community. "Too many of our veterans find themselves on the streets and with limited resources," Matthies said. "In 2018, we saw over one hundred homeless veterans come through our doors.

No matter what the cause or what is going on politically, we are happy to be part of the solution to veteran homelessness."

Today, SVdP Phoenix offers a series of programs to aid the poor, a growth that is owed largely to the seriousness with which SVdP Phoenix takes Frederic Ozanam's admonition, "No work of charity is foreign to the society." SVdP Phoenix feeds the poor through its kitchen and dining rooms, stocks itself from its food warehouse and food reclamation programs, raises food on its urban farms and sponsors the Dream Center and the One at a Time scholarship program. Clothing is provided through its thrift stores, housing is provided through Ozanam Manor and the Resource Center and better health is provided through the medical and dental clinics, the Family Wellness Program and St. Anne's Ministry.

More than 4,500 kitchen-prepared meals are provided daily through the society's five dining rooms, and they are provided free of charge to more than twenty nonprofit agencies. The society's Phoenix-area facilities include: Family Evening Meal at the Dan O'Meara Center, Henry Unger Dining Room (HSC), Chris Becker Dining Room in Sunnyslope, Wayne Unruh Dining Room in Mesa and Santa Teresita Dining Room in El Mirage. Anyone who enters one of the society's dining facilities for a meal will be served—no prerequisites need to be met. However, adults must be accompanied by children to receive services at the Family Evening Meal. Hot nutritious meals are provided, as well as clothing, diapers and hygienic needs. Through relationships with partner agencies, the society is able to connect guests to other resources, twelve-step meetings, Bible study and non-denominational Sunday services—quite an advancement compared to the early years, when a few poor people would humbly ring the bell outside St. Mary's Rectory and receive a sandwich.

As previously discussed, food warehousing and food reclamation were established to help furnish food to SVdP Phoenix's conference food pantries located in Catholic parishes throughout northern and central Arizona. The conferences distribute this food to the needy of their communities. Today, truckloads of food donated by grocery stores and community food drives arrive at the Dan O'Meara Center in Phoenix. The items are sorted and measured against the society's strict quality-control standards before they are sent to its kitchen or community-based food pantries. Food acquired through the society's reclamation process with Fry's stores and community food drives, food purchased with monetary donations and perishable donations made by various stores, warehouses and other member food banks finds its way to the poor and those in need. As of the publication date of this book,

Volunteers and staff processing donated food. All donations are quantified, digitized and reviewed by strict rules of acceptance before being distributed.

the Food Reclamation Center is open Tuesday through Friday, 6:30 a.m. to 3:30 p.m., and on Saturday from 6:00 a.m. to noon for the convenience of conferences that may not be able to pick up food during the week.

In 2018, the food warehouse processed approximately 4.5 million pounds of product. Monthly distribution allotments average about 721 pounds per conference. The warehouse program operates on an open policy, always working to improve the communication between the warehouse and the conferences to better serve them. In 2020, Mary Thomas serves as the manager of the Food Reclamation Center.

One of the special members of SVdP Phoenix is Phyllis O'Toole, who, at ninety years of age, is one of the society's oldest volunteers. She is a Vincentian at Most Holy Trinity Church. O'Toole has been volunteering in the society's food bank since it first opened in 1989, but she was volunteering at the first dining room on Washington Street long before she came to the food bank. O'Toole remembers becoming a Vincentian and volunteering at the pantry at her parish in 1977; it was at a time when women were not allowed to hold office. Eventually, O'Toole was elected president of her conference and held that position for two terms. To this day, O'Toole still volunteers at her pantry. "I like doing this, but I don't lift as well as I did." In 2013, O'Toole received

Ninety-year-old Phyllis O'Toole, a SVdP Phoenix member who has volunteered with the Society for over forty years and continues to serve when possible.

the Glennie Scott Award for her dedicated volunteerism. When asked how she felt about winning, she responded, "I feel ninety. I felt my best at fifty, but I'm not ready to quit. You just keep going one day at a time."

- There are now seventeen thrift stores operating within SVdP Phoenix. Three are located in Phoenix; two thrift stores and a food bank are located in Lake Havasu City; and one thrift store each is located in Surprise, Mesa, Chandler, Apache Junction, Bullhead City, Kingman, Cottonwood, Flagstaff, Mayer, Prescott, Payson and Dolan Springs. They serve the dual role of providing clothing and other household items to the poor and raising money for the society. They honor Care Cards, which are SVdP thrift store gift cards. Conferences purchase them for half the price of their value at the store. Clients may also receive vouchers, which are similar to a prescription for a specific item at the store. Conferences are billed by the accounting office at 25 percent of the retail price or 50 percent of the cost of beds and bed frames.

The grand opening of a thrift store in Surprise, Arizona, on October 17, 2013. Pictured are SVdP Phoenix and City of Surprise representatives.

- In 2019, the SVdP Phoenix Virginia G. Piper Medical and Dental Clinic provided 16,504 medical, dental and wellness visits and consultations for uninsured patients. Patients came from 128 zip codes and ranged from ages two to ninety-four.

- The newly renovated medical clinic, which reopened in December 2018, increased its number of exam rooms from five to nine, and it includes a laboratory, procedure room, ophthalmology room, pharmacy and intake area. The clinic is open to anyone who is either uninsured or underinsured. Appointments are made by phone call.

The dental clinic's main goal is to alleviate patients' pain, treat infections and create a more aesthetically pleasing look so that patients can secure jobs and lead healthier, more enjoyable lives. Thanks to a $1-million grant from Delta Dental of Arizona for operations, the dental clinic doubled its operatory space from eight to sixteen chairs. This will significantly increase the number of visits available to dental patients each year. Anyone without dental insurance or who is underinsured is eligible for dental help. Admission is granted by lottery; thirty applications are available per month. In emergencies, for pain or infection control, clients can sometimes make same-day appointments.

The Family Wellness Program focuses on diabetes prevention and management to help the underserved and uninsured understand their disease and learn how to prevent future complications. The program includes one-on-one counseling, onsite groups for adults and offsite outreach to youth. Adults or children who are diagnosed with or at risk of diabetes are eligible to participate in the program. Classes are given in English and Spanish, and they vary in length from three months to one year. St. Anne's Ministry loans medical equipment, including walkers, crutches and wheelchairs. The availability of this equipment is limited only by the amount of donations received.

There are many stories about how the society's medical and dental clinics have changed lives and created new, positive directions for individuals. This book will look at only two of the myriads of stories of how SVdP Phoenix has made a difference. Picture a ten-year-old girl who looks in the mirror every day and can't help but feel defined by a fine scar running from her top lip to her nose—a cleft lip that had been stitched together when she was a baby but never properly repaired. Her teeth are haphazard, with a gap in the front left by a tooth that had traveled up into her gum and settled there. Her family is uninsured and unsure of where to seek dental attention. Now, think of Teresa, a thirty-seven-year-old mother of five who is experiencing odd abdominal pain, later diagnosed as cervical cancer. She is also uninsured and unsure of where to seek medical attention. It's cases like these that medical and dental professionals at the Virginia G. Piper Medical and Dental Clinic see daily as they act as the healthcare safety net of Maricopa County. Under the dental clinic leadership of Dr. Ken Snyder, Dr. Scott Myers and chief medical officer Dr. Maurice Lee, the on-campus clinic restores hope, health and dignity to the thousands of uninsured and low-income people who are in need of dental and medical services.

Dr. Snyder never forgot that ten-year-old girl and the tears that streamed from her eyes when he told her they would be able to provide her with the braces that would fix her teeth. "The severity of the cases we see in a month here is what a private practice sees in ten years," shared Dr. Snyder. For Dr. Lee, the thirty-seven-year-old mother with cancer's story exemplifies the importance of the free, life-saving services received at SVdP Phoenix and partner organizations that assisted in her diagnosis and eventual

Dr. Maurice Lee, chief medical officer at SVdP Phoenix, consulting with wound care director Dr. Erin Tharalson in the expanded medical center, which was opened in 2018.

treatment plan. Without this resource, Teresa's cancer likely would have gone undiagnosed until it was incurable. The Virginia G. Piper Medical and Dental Clinic is a last resort for many. Thanks to the hard work and dedication of its medical and dental teams, life-changing stories like these are told every day.

The Resource Center houses the homeless ministries and supporting partners. It offers weather relief, food, clothing, showers, hygiene products, haircuts, hot breakfasts and sack lunches. Homelessness prevention measures, such as rental, mortgage and utility assistance, are also offered. The Traveler's Aid Center and representatives of the Department of Economic Security, which can offer help through food stamps, AHCCS (Medicaid) and cash assistance, are housed here. Legal aid is available four days a week. The new building increased the number of men's bathrooms from ten to fourteen, women's bathrooms from two to four (men are much more likely to need services than women) and added one family bathroom with a shower and tub.

As previously stated, the Phoenix Council celebrated its fifty-year anniversary in 1969 and its sixty-year anniversary in 2006. It is understandable that members of any organization to want to acknowledge milestones of time, but surely it is expected when one is acknowledging an organization with such unbelievable success as SVdP Phoenix. In 2019,

SVdP Phoenix San Francisco de Asis conference members cutting the ribbon to celebrate fifty years of service to the Flagstaff, Arizona, community on August 8, 2019.

District One and one of its conferences celebrated milestones of time: the San Francisco Peaks District, located in northern Arizona, celebrated its fifty-year anniversary, and the Immaculate Conception Conference, located in Cottonwood, celebrated its twenty-year anniversary.

In the establishment of conferences, St. Mary's in Phoenix was the first, soon followed by St. Agnes and St. Francis Xavier, both within the city of Phoenix. As if lighting a match, the society's fire soon took off, and other conferences within the Greater Phoenix area soon followed. It was not until 1969, however, that the fire jumped the boundaries of Phoenix and a conference was established in the Flagstaff area, approximately 150 miles north of Phoenix. In the mid- to late 1960s, a group of Knights of Columbus from the Flagstaff local council decided they wanted to start a conference in Flagstaff with the support of three pastors: Reverend Eugene McCarthy from Nativity of Blessed Virgin Mary (BVM), Reverend James E. Lindenmeyer from Our Lady of Guadalupe and Reverend Harry Deering from St. Pius X. This first conference was led by its president Lou Bader. The other officers elected were Elmer Armijo, George McCullough and Robert Dagger. Father Cuthbert Micali served as the conference's spiritual advisor. The conference was formally aggregated as the Pope John XXIII

Conference in August 1969. At the time, Flagstaff's parishes were part of the Diocese of Gallup; later in 1969, the Diocese of Phoenix was formed, which included Flagstaff and much of northern Arizona.

The Pope John XXIII Conference in Flagstaff opened its first thrift store in 1977, at 615 West Santa Fe Street. The location was moved to 2109 East Cedar Street in 1985, and in 1994, it moved again to its current location at 2113 North East Street. In 2008, after the merger of three conferences into the San Francisco de Asis Conference, the current location of the thrift store underwent a significant expansion, providing space for a food pantry, meeting room, helpline office and expanded storage for the store. This expansion was a major change in how the conference operated, and it allowed for the consolidation of most of the conference's activities. Around this same time, SVdP Phoenix partnered with Catholic Charities and began operating its Transient Aid Center (TAC) activities out of the offices of Catholic Charities, which continues to this day.

The Immaculate Conception Conference in Cottonwood was officially established when it received its letter of aggregation in 1999. Ray Hunter served as its first president. The Immaculate Conception Conference serves the communities of Cottonwood, Verde Villages, Clarkdale, Jerome and Cornville. Today, the conference has a roster of over eighty-one members and volunteers; it has no paid employees. In 2019, the members and volunteers of the Immaculate Conception Conference were projected to have worked for about sixteen thousand hours and driven approximately fifty thousand miles in service to the conference. The growth of the Cottonwood conference is a tribute to the unceasing devotion of time, energy and sincere friendship shared by dedicated members and volunteers with those who are in need.

In the early years of this conference, there were several locations in Cottonwood where the Immaculate Conception Conference distributed food and attempted to start a thrift store. During these early years, the conference also transitioned from a loosely bonded group of volunteers who wanted to help people, to a more organized, professional membership of SVdP Phoenix. In 2009, the conference began holding thrift sales regularly three days a month at the old Immaculate Conception Parish Rectory, where food was also being stored. In 2017, a larger vacant facility offered a favorable lease; after some remodeling, all of the conference's operations were moved to the new facility, where the thrift shop is now open for business four days a week. The shop collects donations six days a week and operates a truck for weekly pickup and delivery service. The conference's food pantry now distributes food boxes every Monday and Thursday morning. The food comes from parish donations, SVdP Phoenix, local food banks and supermarkets. Special annual events include the annual Turkey Tuesday Drive for Thanksgiving and a "40 Cans for 40 Days" food drive for Easter.

Another notable conference that was able to expand its services during this period was the St. Germaine Conference in Prescott Valley, Arizona. In 2018, a very generous estate was donated to the conference. This gift allowed it to purchase a larger facility and two buildings located just off church grounds. The site had been a large mechanical facility and required major remodeling and renovation to bring it into the twenty-first century. The first of the two buildings became the administration building, which included a front office for phones and filing, a conference business office for computers and data entry and a meeting space. The second building included a receiving area for semi-trucks bringing food from SVdP Phoenix's Food Reclamation Center and local food banks. It also included space for a full pantry area for food storage, an office and work area for the pantry manager and a break room for pantry workers. It should also be noted that the St. Germaine Conference started in 1987, and its first president was Eugene "Pete" Pike, who served St. Vincent de Paul for thirty-three years. This exceptional conference started with eight members; today, there are forty-seven members and thirty-four associate members.

Another important program that has been hugely beneficial to the education of Phoenix-area youth is the One at a Time scholarship program (OAAT). This program was started in 2001 and continues to provide a way to end generational poverty by financially assisting students who cannot afford college. The success of the program is the result of many factors, especially the assignment of a mentor to each student. One cannot understate the importance of having an experienced adult providing advice and direction to a student.

The program was started by former SVdP Phoenix president Terry Wilson. As of 2019, thirty students were enrolled in the program. There have been seventy-five students who have participated in the scholarship program who have completed an associate or bachelor's degree with an overall college graduation rate of 71 percent. The program supports a diverse student population, including single mothers and scholars who may be experiencing incarceration. Each candidate is required to fill out an application, which is reviewed by the OAAT Scholarship Committee. As part of the application process, each potential candidate is interviewed; once they are accepted into the program, they are introduced at the June general membership meeting. Each student submits a renewal application annually

Marcelino Quiñonez, recipient of a One at a Time scholarship.

in May to continue to receive assistance. Candidates are recommended from many sources, but most are recommended by high school counselors who screen student candidates based on their motivation, academic strengths, ability to complete college and financial need.

To see how the OAAT scholarship program can change lives, one needs to only look at the story of Marcelino Quiñonez. The Quiñonez family immigrated to the United States from Mexico when Marcelino was five years old. He was one of five children, and his parents struggled to support the family. In 2002, Quiñonez graduated from South Mountain High School. He wanted to attend college but could not afford the cost of higher education. He applied for an OAAT scholarship and was accepted into the program. Because of this scholarship program, mentorship and his hard work, he graduated from Arizona State University (ASU) in 2007, becoming the first of his family to graduate from college and inspiring his younger siblings to earn their degrees—Erika Quiñonez graduated in 2008, and Braulio Quiñonez graduated in 2010. Marcelino Quiñonez later earned a master's degree. He became a teacher and was later elected to the Roosevelt School District governing board of directors, and he ran in the primaries for a position in the state legislature. Today, Quiñonez is employed at ASU as the director of educational outreach and partnerships.

The OAAT program is part of SVdP Phoenix's commitment to creating systemic change, and it strives to break the cycle of generational or situational poverty by helping people realize their true human potential, as opposed to relying on others for basic needs. Through this policy directive, efforts are directed toward moving individuals from poverty to sustainability. It is as Anne Isabella Ritchie once stated in 1885, "You can give a man a fish and you feed him for a day; teach a man to fish and you feed him forever." Is it not better to teach one how to fish? Being a fisherman now converts a person living in poverty to a person who has a sustainable life. Many of SVdP's programs were developed with systemic change as a goal. The OAAT program is one of the programs that can help move individuals out of poverty. Marcelino Quiñonez is a beautiful example of systemic change at work. His education opened the door to his success, offering him an opportunity for a better life.

Another point of pride for the society is the continued success of SVdP Cuernavaca. Today, SVdP Cuernavaca is a major community organization and is much like many of the SVDP councils in the United States. Many factors have contributed to the remarkable growth of SVdP in Cuernavaca. Through the years, support from SVdP Phoenix, its districts, conferences and individual members has been critical. The intercambio program has fostered relationships, provided creative ideas for services in Cuernavaca and maintained support from SVdP Phoenix for SVdP Cuernavaca's programs.

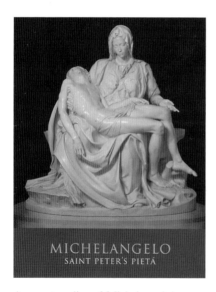

An exact replica of Michelangelo's Pieta, located on the Human Services Campus at 1075 West Jackson Street, Phoenix, Arizona, inside the Henry Unger Dining Room.

The initiative shown by members of SVdP Cuernavaca to serve the poor by enlisting community resources with limited support of the church in Cuernavaca has been remarkable.

It should be emphasized that, while SVdP Phoenix provides a full array of charitable services, it is also a Catholic spiritual organization. Near the end of 2013, guests receiving meals at the Henry Unger Dining Room, located at 1075 West Jackson Street, were given a special gift: an exact replica of Michelangelo's *Pieta* was donated by a very kind gentleman who had visited the facility. His desire was for people who would never have had the opportunity to travel to Rome to experience the beauty and reverence of the sculpture not only as a symbol of the Catholic faith, but as one of the greatest pieces of art ever created. Bishop Thomas J. Olmsted dedicated and blessed the statue after its installation. He was quoted as saying, "For the people that come in here, come with wounds, some of them very fresh, wondering if they can be healed; this will provide a great place for them to pray. This is where wounds are healed." Executive director Steve Zabilski also spoke at the event, saying, "What is often heard is that the most difficult part of being homeless is in not being seen, in becoming invisible. For these people who feel broken, they can see Jesus and Mary when they were broken. They get to see something very moving in this piece of art." A team from the Phoenix Art Museum helped create an appropriate setting for the installation. Visitors are welcome to visit the chapel to see, experience and touch it 7 days a week, 365 days a year.

For years, Arizona Public Service (APS) and Salt River Project (SRP) created minimal assistance programs that were available to all their customers. During this period, SVdP Phoenix regularly paid large utility bills to assist utility customers. Starting in 2014, the Arizona Community Action Agency (ACAA), now called Wildfire, authorized substantial grants to be issued directly to SVdP Phoenix, with the funds to be used to assist utility customers. The grant funding was provided by APS and SRP. SVdP Phoenix evaluates each request for assistance to assure it is legitimate and that basic grant requirements are met. After the completion of the review process, when the client is determined to be eligible, SVdP Phoenix authorizes payment to the identified utility. Since 2014, SVdP Phoenix has received approximately $2 million in utility assistance from APS and SRP, with the vast majority of this assistance provided by APS.

As SVdP Phoenix continues to garner national and worldwide attention, development plans are continually considered for the Phoenix area. The national office of SVdP opened a new fifteen-thousand-square-foot thrift store in Avondale in November 2019. This is the first thrift store to be operated by the National Store Corporation. This prototype store will provide training and allow for the development of the best practices and procedures. The store may provide a model for the future development of new stores throughout the United States.

SVdP is located in more than 150 countries throughout the world and feeds 30 million people every day. On January 19, 2019, Renato Lima de Oliviera, the international president general of the Society of St. Vincent de Paul, visited SVdP Phoenix and shared that it is the largest SVdP council in the world. The president general visited many of the Phoenix facilities and participated in a home visit in the St. Matthew Conference area, one

Board President Attwood, Executive Director Zabilski and staff welcome Renato Lima de Oliviera (*center*), the international president general of the Society of St. Vincent de Paul.

of Phoenix's poorer areas. He was very impressed with what he saw and complimented SVdP Phoenix on all that has been accomplished. He said that the fundamentals are the same throughout the world, but one of the major differences he found in Phoenix was the family atmosphere, where Vincentians work as if they are all part of one family.

7

DISTRICT DEVELOPMENT

Since the implementation of Ron Meyer's district concept in the 1980s, St. Vincent de Paul Phoenix has grown from six to twelve districts. The district designation concept groups at least three conferences together that are similar in location and culture but will not exceed twelve conferences per district. For example, District Seven consists of eight parishes and one special works conference located primarily in South Phoenix with large numbers of minority parishes, and it is strongly influenced by Hispanic parishioners and members. District Eleven, conversely, is located in the northwest area of greater Phoenix and is influenced by retired parishioners and members.

When the districts were first formed, they consisted of just a few conferences and were easy to group together. Today, districts cover seven counties and thirty-eight cities in Arizona. Some districts that were once located in middle-class neighborhoods are now located in impoverished areas, while formerly sparsely populated districts with few conferences are today located in wealthy, populated neighborhoods. The twinning process allows wealthy districts and conferences to distribute resources and assist conferences surrounded by poverty.

Districts meet once a month to discuss issues and concerns within the district area. Every conference within a district tithes 10 percent of their financial donations to the district; any conference in financial need can ask the district for assistance. The president of each conference serves on the district board. The district board officers are selected from the district board, serving as president, vice president, treasurer and secretary.

As of August 2019, the Phoenix Council is composed of twelve districts; in turn, each district consists of several conferences. The twelve districts are listed below, including the conferences in each district, the conference's location and the conference's date of aggregation.

District One: San Francisco Peaks District
- ➤ Immaculate Conception, Cottonwood, Arizona, 1994
- ➤ St. Frances Cabrini, Camp Verde, Arizona, 2009
- ➤ St. John Vianney, Sedona, Arizona, 1987
- ➤ St. Joseph, Williams, Arizona, 2009
- ➤ St. Jude, Tuba City, Arizona, 1996
- ➤ San Francisco de Asis, Flagstaff, Arizona, 1969

District Two: Colorado River District
- ➤ Our Lady of the Desert, Dolan Springs, Arizona, 1993
- ➤ Our Lady of the Lake, Lake Havasu City, Arizona, 1987
- ➤ Sacred Heart, Parker, Arizona, 2002
- ➤ St. Margaret Mary, Bullhead City, Arizona, 1983
- ➤ St. Mary, Kingman, Arizona, 1993

District Three: Our Lady of the Poor District
- ➤ Our Lady of Lourdes, Sun City West, Arizona, 1987
- ➤ St. Anthony of Padua, Wickenburg, Arizona, 1996
- ➤ St. Clare of Assisi, Surprise, Arizona, 2005
- ➤ St. Clement of Rome, Sun City, Arizona, 1998
- ➤ St. Elizabeth Seton, Sun City, Arizona, 1982
- ➤ St. Joachim and St. Anne, Sun City, Arizona, 1965

District Four: Sal Immordino District
- ➤ Our Lady of the Valley, Phoenix, Arizona, 1986
- ➤ St. Helen, Glendale, Arizona, 1985
- ➤ St. James, Glendale, Arizona, 1985
- ➤ St. Jerome, Phoenix, Arizona, 1966
- ➤ St. Joan of Arc, Phoenix, Arizona, 1986
- ➤ St. Joseph, Phoenix, Arizona, 1985
- ➤ St. Paul, Phoenix, Arizona, 1987
- ➤ St. Raphael, Glendale, Arizona, 1983
- ➤ St. Thomas More, Glendale, Arizona, 2003

District Five: Father Eugene Maguire District
- Blessed Sacrament, Scottsdale, Arizona, 1989
- Our Lady of Perpetual Help, Scottsdale, Arizona, 1952
- St. Daniel the Prophet, Scottsdale, Arizona, 1966
- St. Maria Goretti, Scottsdale, Arizona, 1985
- St. Mark, Phoenix, Arizona, 1953
- St. Theresa, Phoenix, Arizona, 1957

District Six: Father Victor Bucher Council
- Most Holy Trinity, Phoenix, Arizona, 1953
- Our Lady of Perpetual Help, Glendale, Arizona, 1951
- St. Agnes, Phoenix, Arizona, 1949
- St. Francis Xavier, Phoenix, Arizona, 1949
- St. Gregory, Phoenix, Arizona, 1951
- St. Louis the King, Glendale, Arizona, 1965
- St. Mary's Basilica, Phoenix, Arizona, 1949
- St. Thomas the Apostle, Phoenix, Arizona, 1952
- Saints Simon and Jude Cathedral, Phoenix, Arizona, 1955

District Seven: Art Whitney Council
- Holy Family, Phoenix, Arizona, 1987
- Sacred Heart, Phoenix, Arizona, 1957
- St. Anthony, Phoenix, Arizona, 1954
- St. Catherine of Siena, Phoenix, Arizona, 1953
- St. Edward the Confessor, Phoenix, Arizona, 1987
- St. John Paul II, Phoenix, Arizona, 1993
- St. Martin de Porres, Phoenix, Arizona, 1982
- St. Matthew, Phoenix, Arizona, 1952
- St. Vincent de Paul, Phoenix, Arizona, 1965

District Eight: Our Lady of Guadalupe Council
- Blessed Sacrament, Tolleson, Arizona, 1985
- St. Augustine, Phoenix, Arizona, 1983
- St. Michael, Gila Bend, Arizona, 2004
- St. Thomas Aquinas, Avondale, Arizona, 1995
- St. William, Cashion, Arizona, 1987

District Nine: Father Joseph Patterson Council
- All Saints, Mesa, Arizona, 1982

- Christ the King, Mesa, Arizona, 1959
- Holy Cross, Mesa, Arizona, 1983
- Our Lady of Guadalupe, Queen Creek, Arizona, 2012
- Queen of Peace, Mesa, Arizona, 1954
- St. Bridget, Mesa, Arizona, 1990
- St. Mary Magdalene, Gilbert, Arizona, 2005
- St. Timothy, Mesa, Arizona, 2007

District Ten: Yavapai County Council
- Sacred Heart, Prescott, Arizona, 1993
- St. Catherine Laboure, Chino Valley, Arizona, 1996
- St. Germaine, Prescott Valley, Arizona, 1989
- St. Joseph, Mayer, Arizona, 1989

District Eleven: St. Elizabeth Seton Council
- Church of the Ascension, Fountain Hills, Arizona, 1989
- Our Lady of Joy, Carefree, Arizona, 1987
- St. Bernadette, Scottsdale, Arizona, 1997
- St. Bernard of Clairvaux, Scottsdale, Arizona, 1999
- St. Gabriel the Archangel, Cave Creek, Arizona, 2009
- Annunciation Catholic School Vibrant Vinnies (Elementary Conference from St. Gabriel Parish), Cave Creek, Arizona, 2017
- St. Philip the Apostle, Payson, Arizona, 1989
- St. Rose Philippine Duchesne/Good Shepherd/St. Philip Benizi, Anthem, Arizona, 1994

District Twelve: Monsignor Daniel McCready Council
- All Saints Newman Center, Arizona State University, Tempe, Arizona, 2009
- Church of the Resurrection, Tempe, Arizona, 1986
- Corpus Christi, Phoenix, Arizona, 1992
- Our Lady of Mt. Carmel, Tempe, Arizona, 1953
- St. Benedict, Phoenix, Arizona, 2003
- St. Mary, Chandler, Arizona, 1987
- St. Steven, Sun Lakes, Arizona, 2010

It should be noted that not all of the district conferences meet the definition of parish conference (a conference made up of adults who are primarily members of a designated parish within the Catholic Diocese of

Phoenix). St. John Paul II is a special ministry conference that is based on the Dan O'Meara Center in Phoenix located on Watkins Road. Another conference that lies outside the normal conference definition is the Vibrant Vinnies Conference, which is primarily made up of junior high students from Annunciation Catholic School and a few neighboring schools. They are the only elementary-level conference in the western region. The conference was started by Ling Patty and was given an aggregation date of June 2017. Patty started the conference as a way to ensure the future growth of SVdP Phoenix.

St. Philip the Apostle, located in Payson, Arizona (Gila County), and St. Jude, located in Tuba City, Arizona (Coconino County), are assigned to the Catholic Diocese of Gallup, New Mexico. Sacred Heart is located in Parker, Arizona (La Paz County), and in the Catholic Diocese of Tucson, Arizona. Although they are not a part of the Catholic Diocese of Phoenix, they are all strong contributing conferences of SVdP Phoenix and do a fantastic job providing assistance to the poor within their jurisdictions. All three conferences are approved fraternal union members.

8

RESPONSE TO CRISES

The board of directors notes that one of the great strengths of SVDP Phoenix is its adaptability. Its response to Hurricane Katrina was an example of that adaptability, as was its reaction to the abrupt closure of a downtown overflow homeless shelter. For two years, from 2016 to 2018, SVdP Phoenix opened its homeless dining room (not the Hall of Banners, which is for families) in the evening and throughout the night to provide emergency housing.

Hurricane Katrina was an extremely destructive and deadly category 5 hurricane that made landfall on Florida and Louisiana in August 2005, causing catastrophic damage, particularly in New Orleans and the surrounding areas. Subsequent flooding happened largely as the result of the failure of the flood control levees that surround the city. The final death toll was 1,836, with scores of individuals left without homes. Government officials were faced with finding shelter for thousands of families and individuals. New Orleans decided to move these people to other cities throughout the country. Phoenix was one of the cities chosen to accept Katrina refugees.

SVdP Phoenix stepped up to help in this humanitarian crisis. The first opportunity to help came the day after the refugees arrived at the Arizona Veterans Memorial Coliseum in Phoenix. That morning, Vincentian Blase Bova, the director of special ministries, and Joe Power, a board member and liaison for the Transient Aid Center (TAC), went to work. Bova, Power and a band of volunteers brought TAC to the coliseum and began helping many of the stranded people by arranging travel, purchasing bus and plane tickets and connecting refugees with friends and relatives. After a few days, when housing vouchers were given to people who wished to remain in Phoenix, TAC and Vincentians from Phoenix conferences assisted many individuals and families with obtaining the things they needed to set up a household. SVdP Phoenix took on the task of caring for and settling the refugees, providing assistance to 1,621 individuals by December 2005. A comment made by one of the Katrina refugees summarizes the catastrophe that this category 5 hurricane imposed on the citizens of the southeastern United States: "My history is gone—my whole life was washed away—I have nothing left—I feel empty inside. I cried every day; I lost everything."

One of the most significant crises SVdP Phoenix faced occurred in 2005 and 2006, when individuals experiencing homelessness were dying from the heat in downtown Phoenix. As previously stated, the SVdP Phoenix dining room is a part of the Human Services Campus (HSC) at Ninth Avenue and Madison Street, but its primary function is to feed people; Central Arizona Shelter Services (CASS) provided sleeping accommodations. The demand, however, was much greater than the CASS capacity. As a result, people were dying on the streets. By the end of July 2005, thirty individuals had died of heat-related causes that summer; the vast majority of them were homeless and without shelter. A July 23, 2005 *New York Times* article that focused on the 2005 summer heat in Phoenix noted: "Daytime highs in Phoenix have remained near 110 degrees for more than a week, and municipal officials acknowledge that it is almost impossible to deal with the needs of the estimated 10,000 to 20,000 people living on the streets. The city has barely 1,000 shelter beds, and hundreds of them are available only in the winter."

During the summers, from 2016 to 2018, one of the dining rooms provided overnight shelter to 250 people; the room was reset daily for breakfast service.

SVdP Phoenix stepped in to find a solution. At the time, the society's downtown Henry Unger Dining Room was serving lunch daily. It decided to open up the lunch area at night as a space for a temporary shelter. With cots donated from the Red Cross and staff working on overtime or shifting schedules, the society was able to accommodate about 100 individuals, mostly men, to keep them out of the heat and provide safe, nightly shelter. It was not unusual to see the senior leadership team helping out in the evenings. For two years, from September 2016 to 2018, SVdP Phoenix ran the overflow shelter in its dining room, accepting about 250 men and women every night. These individuals were treated with respect and provided safe hospitality at night, and they had access to resources and services at the HSC during the day. After the first night of trial and learning with logistics, no one was turned away from the society's shelter for two years.

In December 2017, the collaborative that was providing financial assistance to the temporary shelter began to discuss the fact that the shelter was not meant to be permanent; they wanted to reinvest their funds in permanent housing and long-term solutions. SVdP Phoenix ensured its partners that as long as there was funding and community will, it would continue this multi-use of the dining room. As it turned out, there was neither ongoing funding nor community will.

Again, the community embarked on a plan to shift resources. SVdP Phoenix and its campus partners planned to engage people in the shelter with housing interventions and decrease shelter capacity over time, such that at the end of the contract period, hundreds of people were not left with nowhere to go. Out of the 328 people who were frequent users of the shelter when the closure announcement was made in the spring of 2018, 304 were able to acquire other shelter or housing options or were able to leave the shelter on their own. Even the "last man standing," as he called himself, someone who had been at the overflow shelter for years and would not go into alternative shelter, was able to go into the Ozanam Manor transitional housing program.

Ironically, on October 1, 2018, the first day that the overflow shelter was supposed to be closed, hurricane-like weather led to the opening of the dining room that night for weather relief. Despite the fact that an overflow shelter is no longer funded on an ongoing basis, the need remains. SVdP Phoenix is open to serving where it can in this capacity. Weather-relief emergency shelter continues to this day. On July 23, 2019, with the help of the society's campus partners, 250 individuals slept in the dining room. One of the society's campus partners noted, "St. Vincent de Paul are the

'Yes people.' No problem can't be solved, especially when people's lives are at risk. They definitely modeled the importance of human dignity." As long as it is able, SVdP Phoenix will refuse to let individuals suffer on the street.

Another crisis that required SVdP Phoenix's intervention occurred near the end of 2018. Large numbers of asylum seekers from Central America, largely consisting of families with small children, began arriving at the United States–Mexico border. U.S. Immigration and Customs Enforcement (ICE) can accept asylum seekers and grant them lawful entry into the United States while they follow the legal process to be granted or denied asylum. ICE releases families with legal documentation if they have a family member or host somewhere in the United States who can arrange transportation to reunite them. The families are then assigned to a court in the jurisdiction of their destination to continue the formal asylum process. Once released, most families spend between twenty-four and seventy-two hours in Arizona until transportation can be arranged to take them to their final destination. From October 2018 to April 2019, approximately fifteen thousand people, half of whom were children, came through the Phoenix area and were supported by churches and volunteer groups that quietly provided food and shelter and arranged for transportation to the asylum seekers' final destinations with virtually no government or outside support.

Initially, the number of people released by ICE was small, but it quickly increased to two hundred or more per day. As such, ICE often released families at the Greyhound bus station or elsewhere in the community with only the clothes on their backs and no way to contact family to make transportation arrangements. The families arrived exhausted, many did not speak English, some had health issues, they had no money and many had experienced violence or trauma. The flow of released families far exceeded the capacity of the volunteer network to support them, and the community was desperate to find a more permanent and sustainable solution to this human crisis.

In response, SVdP Phoenix began piloting a "day relief center" for asylum-seeking families in partnership with the International Rescue Committee (IRC), providing a safe haven, hospitality, food, clothes and play areas for the children. SVdP Phoenix placed these families in the Dan O'Meara Dining Hall and found ways to fit this program into its regular dining activities. The society provided a safe haven for these families while its partners took on the logistical coordination of travel and overnight lodging. After an initial pilot weekend (Friday, March 22, to Sunday, March 24, 2019) the day relief center opened on Tuesday, March 26, 2019, and continued to run six days a week.

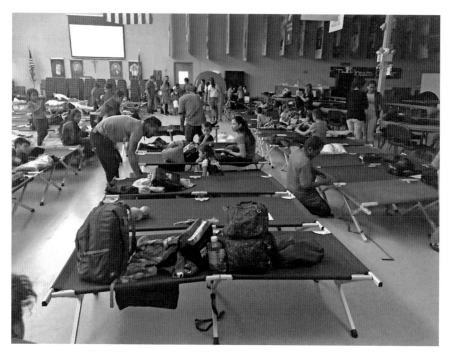

Between October 2018 and April 2019, temporary shelter and assistance was provided to approximately fifteen thousand asylum seekers released into the Phoenix area.

SVdP Phoenix is committed to providing as much assistance as possible in this humanitarian relief effort, and it strongly supports community efforts to find a long-term, sustainable solution.

The Rodeo-Chediski Wildfire burned in eastern Arizona beginning on June 22, 2002, and was not brought under control until July 7, 2002. It burned 468,638 acres and was classified as the worst wildfire in Arizona history to that time. Several local communities, including Show Low, Pinetop-Lakeside, Heber-Overguard, Clay Springs and Pinedale, were threatened and had to be evacuated. The Rodeo-Chediski fire was generally located outside of the society's diocesan council area, but through its nearby Payson Conference, SVdP Phoenix provided substantial assistance.

As reported previously, St. Vincent de Paul in Cuernavaca, Mexico (SVdP Cuernavaca) is closely aligned with Phoenix, and in one instance, it responded courageously to a catastrophic crisis. In 2017, a major earthquake occurred in areas in the eastern part of Morelos, including parts of Cuernavaca. Within ten hours of the earthquake, SVdP Cuernavaca mobilized to collect relief supplies. Scores of students who were out of school due to the crisis volunteered to prepare emergency supply kits for displaced families. SVdP Cuernavaca followed up by affiliating with organizations to rebuild houses and purchase equipment for small businesses.

There have been numerous communities and national crises that SVdP Phoenix has responded to, but there have also been internal crises that have had to be dealt with. One such crisis occurred in Prescott, Arizona, when the Sacred Heart Conference food pantry was destroyed by a fire just nine days before Christmas in 2003. The food pantry was located a short distance from the Sacred Heart Catholic Church in Prescott. The local Sacred Heart Conference had prepared a list of individuals and families who were to receive food for their Christmas dinners and toys for the children, but the fire destroyed everything that they had anticipated giving out to the needy. For the members of the Sacred Heart Conference, it was to be their worst Christmas ever. However, local and Phoenix news outlets reported the story of the fire, and the response was unbelievable. The store manager of the local Fry's food market personally delivered food to conference members and told them to call if they were short on anything. Conference members worked tirelessly in the parish school gym to ensure that the food boxes were properly prepared and distributed. Monetary donations, along with food and stuffed toys, poured in. Despite the tragedy of the fire, no one went without a Christmas dinner.

During the period after the fire, conference members could not keep up with all the offers of help. A parish priest brought in a $1,000 donation from an emergency fund; clients offered labor; Sacred Heart Parish accepted phone calls and accompanying donations; Catholic Social Services provided additional phone coverage and allowed temporary operations in their conference room. One of the donations included a small red box with rolled coins and dollars that were obviously from someone's piggy bank. Two high-school girls from Phoenix who had seen the news coverage raised $150 at a garage sale. The heavy news coverage of the fire caught the attention of Mike Gausden, the western region manager of Hunt Construction, who offered to help rebuild the pantry. Hunt Construction donated the labor and helped secure the donated material needed to rebuild the pantry. Sue Godbold, president of the Sacred Heart Conference at the time, made the following comment: "We were able to witness the miracle of God's love repeatedly through the many donations we received, as well as from the spirit of cooperation between our conference and the community to get us back up and running. Our God is an awesome God, and the Sacred Heart Conference is stronger for being tested by fire."

9

USE OF COMMITTEES

S t. Vincent de Paul Phoenix created functional committees to better coordinate and work out issues of concern. These committees were usually composed of both staff and Vincentian members, and they always had a designated liaison with the board of directors. The idea was to have the committees work out minor details or develop policy that would be brought to the board of directors or the general membership for approval.

There have been many programs, committees and subcommittees created over the society's seventy-four years of service to the community. This chapter will concentrate on the existing committees and explain their functions. These special committees have been extremely successful.

BUDGET COMMITTEE: The adoption of bylaws in September 1988 maintained functions that were performed by committees within the structure of the council. The bylaws mandated the adoption of a budget before each fiscal year with the provision that "the entire budget or any item of the budget cannot be exceeded unless the council votes to amend the budget" (article VI, section 3). The existing budget process was continued; the treasurer was the budget committee chairperson, and they were responsible for the budget process. The budget committee reviewed each department's budget; the resulting budget was submitted to the board of directors for modification, approval and submission to the conference presidents at a general membership meeting for final approval.

By 2000, the executive director and director of finance were preparing a preliminary budget that was presented to the budget committee for review and further development by the subcommittees.

On June 14, 2008, the diocesan council approved a new set of bylaws. Under the new bylaws, the treasurer (article XXVII: Officers: Treasurer/ Chief Financial Officer) continued to oversee the preparation of the budget.

By 2009, the administrative staff and operations at the Dan O'Meara Center had grown to such a degree that the chief financial officer had assumed the task of preparing the budget and submitting it to the budget committee for review and comment. The budget committee forwarded its findings in a preliminary budget to the board for initial approval. The approved budget was presented to conferences by the chief financial officer at the district meetings, and questions and additional proposals were considered. After the district and budget committee review, the board approved the final budget and submitted it to conference presidents at the general membership meeting each September. This system is currently used.

FINANCE ADVISORY COMMITTEE: By 1995, a finance advisory committee had been established with several objectives. It was the committee's responsibility to review and propose an annual budget to the board of directors. Its other objectives included acting as a resource for the director of finance to oversee budget implementation, to review investment policies, review insurance coverage and oversee the annual audit and present the audit to the board. The advisory committees attached to departments (facilities, food services, stores/warehouse, volunteer services and Ministry to the Homeless and Incarcerated and their Families) were to assist the departments in the preparation and review of their annual budgets.

When it was created in the 1990s, the finance advisory committee reviewed funds set aside as endowments for SVdP Phoenix. Initially, all endowment funds were kept as certificates of deposit in local banks. Some of the board members were reluctant at first to place endowment funds in equity markets, fearing that the endowment funds could decrease in value in times of market downturn. However, the receipt of large endowments and an increase in board funds required counsel from outside investment consulting services.

The board initially used the Phoenix Diocesan Financial Advisory Committee to review and propose the allocation of invested funds for optimum returns. In time, an independent investment committee was formed to work with the executive director to investigate investment advisory services. After an evaluation of investment advisors, Buckingham Financial Advisors, based in St. Louis, Missouri, was hired to assist the executive director and Investment Committee. Today, the board's investment committee meets with Buckingham semiannually to set goals and policies for endowment, board-restricted and other operating funds. Budget, audit and investment review functions are currently placed with the finance advisory committee.

AUDIT COMMITTEE: Under article XXXIII of the 2008 bylaws, the treasurer was given the responsibility of conducting an annual audit and appointing members to the audit committee. The audit of SVdP Phoenix's financial records must be completed within 180 days of the end of the fiscal year. The audit committee reviews the annual audit that is completed by an independent certified public accounting firm. Recommendations are prepared by the committee and forwarded to the auditor and executive director.

In May 2012, the newly adopted district bylaws mandated that an annual audit be made of district finances within 180 days of the end of the fiscal year. These audits may be prepared by a CPA firm or prepared by administrative staff or committees appointed by district presidents. On September 16, 2014, newly adopted conference bylaws mandated reviews for all conferences. These reviews may be performed by administrative staff members or persons selected from other conferences in cooperation with conference treasurers.

GOVERNANCE COMMITTEE: A charter for a governance committee for SVdP Phoenix was approved by the board on January 4, 2013. On September 20, 2017, the charter was amended and is still in effect today. The committee was charged with reviewing how the board operated and making recommendations for greater efficiency. A board retreat was approved, and the board voted to hold it annually. Retreats have included participating in a poverty simulation, developing a long-range plan, developing a better working relationship between the board and conferences and board self-evaluation. Each retreat begins with mass and continues until mid-afternoon. During these retreats, some committee accomplishments have included changing how district presidents and committee chairs report to the board, changing the board agenda to shorten meetings and establishing committee charters for all active committees. The governance committee meets once a month.

CONFERENCE RESOURCES COMMITTEE: As part of the organizational efforts implemented by President Terry Wilson, the conference resources and concerns committee was created in 1991; Tom Clouser was appointed chairman. Clouser served as chairman until he was replaced by Ray Daoust in 2018. Shirley Smalley became chairwoman of what is now called the conference resources committee (CRC) in 2019. She is responsible for the nine districts in the Phoenix metropolitan area; Mary Ann Hunter chairs the CRC, serving the three districts in northern Arizona.

The committee was created to identify and develop potential resources that could be used by SVdP Phoenix. It also attempted to identify and resolve potential problems that could negatively impact SVdP Phoenix. Clouser and Daoust also served as members of the board of directors, providing a liaison between the committee and the board. The chairmen of the twinning and spirituality committees were also members of the conference resources committee. These were not subcommittees as such; however, this membership allowed these committees to have a liaison presence with the board of directors.

On the resources side of the equation, several important policy documents were developed by the committee. The first of these documents was a how-to manual, "How to Run a Conference." The development of this document took several years to complete, and when it was finished, it was made available to all members and conferences. Another important project of the committee was to develop a one- or two-page summary on issues and programs of importance to SVdP Phoenix. These short policy statements offered practical guidance and suggestions for conference operation, and they were to be made available to all members of SVdP Phoenix. Their primary purpose was to provide clarity and direction to members. These summary documents were called "bricks" and were continuously revised; new bricks were developed as the need arose. In 2020, thirty-four bricks were available and could be found on the SVdP Phoenix website. The committee also reviews capital asset requests submitted by conferences and administers twinning funds.

The concerns aspect of the equation was less documented but just as important as the resources part of the committee's role. Issues of concern were identified and brought before the committee for discussion and for corresponding development of recommended solutions. Tom Clouser usually involved himself and attempted to work with both sides of the controversy. There were times that Clouser was able to resolve the problem; other times, he would bring the issue to the SVdP Phoenix executive committee for its consideration. Clouser did an admirable job trying to resolve controversial issues and often found himself in the middle of a hail storm. His patience and composure are to be commended.

The working relationship between Vincentian support services and the committee members was excellent and no doubt accounts for much of the great success of this committee.

Voice of the Poor Committee: The society's national office initiated the Voice of the Poor under the society's International Rule VII: "Relationship with civil society, work for social justice" (April 2005). This initiative is based on the recognition by Vincentians that poverty is the result of multiple factors negatively impacting lives and the desire to advocate to "end poverty through systemic change." The society gives immediate help but also seeks mid-term and long-term solutions.

Over the course of the past two decades, Voice of the Poor committees have been created by SVdP councils across the country, from Long Island, New York, to San Francisco. Over time, the national Voice of the Poor committee developed position papers on various topics related to poverty. These papers, approved by the SVdP national council, form the foundation for advocacy by Voice of the Poor. Position papers can be found on the SVdP national Voice of the Poor website. Their topics include healthcare for the poor, affordable housing, education, homelessness, human trafficking, hunger, immigration, predatory lending, fair wages, self-sufficient wages and restorative justice. Also available on the website are numerous Voice of the Poor committee workshop presentations and webinars.

The SVdP Phoenix Voice of the Poor was one of the earliest and most active committees. The goal of the Phoenix Voice of the Poor committee was to have at least one representative as a contact in the parishes with SVdP conferences. For twelve years, Voice of the Poor, led by Kathy Jorgensen, fought harmful predatory loans, known as "payday loans," with potential of triple-digit interest rates that frequently created a debt trap for low-income families. Jorgensen was joined in this effort by Vincentians from Tucson and other cities across the United States. She became known nationally for her advocacy in this area.

For many years, representatives from SVdP Phoenix Voice of the Poor attended the United States Catholic Conference of Bishops' annual Social Ministry Gathering in Washington, D.C. Regular attendees included Lucy Howell, Inge Casey, Frank Barrios, Ron Meyer, Steve Jenkins, Julie Douglas, Father William J. Fitzgerald and Kathy Jorgensen. The group has visited all Arizona congressional offices on Capitol Hill, presenting the United States Conference of Catholic Bishops' position papers on pending national legislation as well as an Arizona agenda approved by SVdP Phoenix. The society's issues included a request for additional section 8 vouchers for Arizona and immigration reform. The society quickly learned that the real work in congressional offices is done by bright, energetic twenty-somethings. Every year, it looked forward to the performance by the "Capitol Steps," whose quick wit and imitations of well-known politicians was most entertaining. One year, Tim Russert came to speak to the society as fellow Catholics concerned with social justice.

Lucy Howell served on the national Voice of the Poor committee for many years, presenting Voice of the Poor as an advocacy option at national and mid-year meetings in Chicago, Indianapolis, Austin, San Diego, Phoenix, Anaheim, Tucson and St. Louis. She chaired Voice of the Poor for the western region for several years, and she was succeeded by Giulio Grecchi of the Tucson SVdP council, who continued Howell's work, expanding on her relationships across the region. For about seven years, Grecchi was the author of an excellent bimonthly newsletter for Voice of the Poor western region, a giant step in communication for the ten-state region. In addition, he built a regional Voice of the Poor website and organized monthly conference calls, bringing together Voice of the Poor representatives of the most active locations in the region.

Voice of the Poor has continued to grow with active committees across the United States. The national Voice of the Poor chair is Jack Murphy of Atlanta, who is also a national board member. In 2020, the Voice of the Poor western region chair is Dan Torrington of Tucson. SVdP Phoenix's Voice of the Poor committee continues to meet monthly, and it is chaired by Ron Meyer, with Father William Fitzgerald serving as its chaplain.

Phoenix lost a clarion voice in 2018 with the passing of Kathy Jorgensen. It is not possible to think of Voice of the Poor without thinking of her. (If advocacy is needed in Heaven, Kathy is doing it!)

TWINNING COMMITTEE: Per the way the districts were structured, encompassing areas of similarity, Districts Seven and Eight were made up of poor conferences in Catholic parishes that were struggling to financially survive. These were areas where the need for SVdP Phoenix's services was the greatest, yet resources were the most limited there.

The SVdP Phoenix theory is that needed resources for the parish conference should come from parish members, but when the parish is poor and the need is great, the conference is seriously underfunded. If the district is also underfunded, the conference will be in serious financial trouble, hence the creation of the concept of "twinning," whereby financial aid is provided to struggling conferences, providing them with a regular income. The term "twinning" has also been used to include all types of outside assistance. Some conferences have provided members to help with conference responsibilities or have provided additional food supplies.

Traditionally, the twinning committee met once a year, usually in January, to review the annual reports of conferences requesting twinning assistance. Conferences selected for assistance received a check every three months with the receipt of the check dependent on conference compliance with SVdP Phoenix regulations. If they were not in compliance, no check would be sent for that three-month period. Once actions were corrected and the conference was again in compliance, financial distributions would resume.

In 2020, Shirley Smalley became the chairperson of the twinning committee. After an evaluation of the role of the committee and the processes in place, the committee has been taking steps to improve its efficiency and determine areas where needs are the greatest. A tighter interview process has been established, using more analysis than before. In addition, a resource guide is being developed that will help conferences find new avenues for financial support. The processes are evolving, and when they are completed, they will surely provide better financial assistance resources to struggling conferences. The name of the committee has been changed to the council aid and twinning committee to better reflect its role. The committee will continue to meet once a year, holding additional meetings as needed, and distribute assistance checks every three months.

OZANAM MANOR COMMITTEE: This committee is charged with reviewing the written and oral operations reports concerning Ozanam Manor's financial services and client outcome progress. Information is provided both by the program director and the staff. Committee members are expected to ensure that they understand the information and are able to take part in relevant discussions and make recommendations to improve the program. The committee meets on a quarterly basis at the Ozanam Manor facility; an Ozanam Manor liaison makes regular written reports to SVdP Phoenix's board of directors. In 2020, the current chairperson of the Ozanam Manor Committee is Jeanne O'Brien. Previous chairpersons have included Don Hieple, Bill Melby and Dick Kowalski.

FOOD SERVICES COMMITTEE: The Food Services Committee began in 1988; at that time, it was named the operations advisors committee food services and was created in order to coordinate the way SVdP Phoenix would operate with Fry's stores to reclaim donated food items. Since then, the committee has been renamed the food services committee. In 2010, the committee began meeting monthly and consisted of food service managers and directors; Sharon Sammartino is the chairperson.

The food services committee also provides a forum that allows managers and directors to discuss challenges, accomplishments and current projects. One of the goals of this committee is to share information between the dining rooms, kitchen, reclamation center and conferences and to advise staff and evaluate policies affecting food service operations. The committee's objectives are to assist in carrying out the long-range plans set forth by the board of directors, help with budget preparation and review policy, procedures and capital equipment needs.

SPIRITUALITY COMMITTEE: The history of this committee is thoroughly covered in Chapter 4. A major part of the recent efforts of this committee has involved Ozanam Formation Experience (OFE) training. In general, there has been a continuing effort to teach SVdP history and what is expected of members. There is also an increased effort to teach members about personal spirituality and how people view themselves as members of SVdP Phoenix. These OFE classes emphasize, "Yes, we are called to serve, but how do we respond to that call?"

The restructured spirituality committee wished to increase the spirituality of all Vincentians in SVdP Phoenix. On November 15, 2014, this committee offered a special half-day class at the Franciscan Renewal Center. The session was taught by the society's own Vincentians and covered spirituality, prayer and judgmentalism. Conference presidents and spiritual advisors attended in the hope of gaining a "trickle down" refocus on the spiritual side of being a Vincentian. The session was well received. During this restructuring period, Vincentians began giving OFE classes. The classes were given in both English and Spanish. In 2007, Jim Prendergast became chairperson of the committee, later followed by Amy Rodriguez. In 2020, the chairperson is Mary Ann Hunter, a Vincentian from Flagstaff.

SERVE OUR STORES COMMITTEE: The stores committee is one of the oldest committees established by St. Vincent de Paul in Phoenix. Over the years, this committee has been known by many different names but has always existed to provide direction in the running of the thrift stores. In 1950, Louis Oliger was appointed as the first chairman of the stores committee. At that time, it was called the salvage committee.

At first, the thrift stores were run by SVdP Phoenix members and volunteers. When the society was small, this arrangement worked well, but as it expanded and new stores opened, this arrangement became less profitable, and the society even considered closing some of its thrift stores. It started hiring store managers instead of using volunteer managers and finally hired a head store manager to oversee the operations of the thrift stores.

In 2008, president Joe Riley (2008–2014) created the Serve Our Stores committee, into which the stores committee was folded. Riley appointed then-board vice president Shirley Smalley as chair of the newly created committee. One of its first initiatives was a concerted effort to secure more volunteers to assist in the running of the thrift stores. After four years, Smalley was succeeded as committee chair by Joann Prendergast. This committee was instrumental in improving the thrift stores. In 2020, Bill Day chairs the Serve Our Stores committee. Mike McClanahan is the director of retail operations.

10

PARTNERSHIPS AND VOLUNTEERS

S t. Vincent de Paul Phoenix has one of the greatest volunteer programs in Arizona. Every day, it is contacted by individuals, families and corporations wishing to volunteer to provide services to those in need. Visit any of the society's facilities, and you will find people wearing SVdP aprons, hats and shirts, providing a myriad of services—anything from making peanut butter and jelly sandwiches to serving food to our guests or identifying canned goods being digitized in our warehouse. Many volunteers enjoy working in the society's thrift stores, while doctors and dentists volunteer at its medical and dental clinics.

Many individuals and corporations provide financial assistance to SVdP Phoenix. It would be impossible to list all of those who financially support the society. A large sign is found in the Hall of Banners showing logos of a large number of its corporate partners. The list is far from complete. No doubt, the society has a large donor base that believes in what it does. The Board of Directors has praise for all of the partnerships that enable SVdP Phoenix to reach out to the poor. Some provide direct assistance in the society's mission to help those in need, while others provide resources to help develop infrastructure so that it can better assist others. Executive director Steve Zabilski said:

> One of the great things about being on our team at St. Vincent de Paul here in Phoenix is seeing God's generous providence to our work. Don't get me wrong, there are hundreds of great community and faith-based

A sign in the Hall of Banners at the Dan O'Meara Center reflecting the logos of some of the organizations that support SVdP Phoenix.

Young students volunteering at the dental clinic. Dr. Ken Snyder is standing on the far right.

organizations all across Arizona. We partner with dozens of them, and I'm certain that God's grace helps them all, too. But all I can tell you is that I can see His generosity and care for us literally every day, and nearly always, it comes wrapped in the kindness and care of our friends and neighbors.

In the spring of 2019, observers did not need to look any further than SVdP Phoenix's north parking lot—usually full of cars owned by Vincentians, dedicated volunteers and employees—to see an example of Zabilski's words. In this case, providence acted through the neighborly foresight and resolve of Arizona Public Service Company (APS), Arizona's largest public utility, to do what any observer would call "a mighty work." SVdP Phoenix's main lot is now home to 144 parking spaces, all covered by APS solar panels that generate more than forty kilowatt hours each day and help improve Arizona's renewable-energy efforts while lowering the society's electric bill. "We are so thrilled and so grateful for this project," noted Zabilski. "This is literally a million-dollar project for APS, and with our focus on serving economically challenged families, we could never have afforded such an investment. What APS has done is a miracle in every way.

Arizona Public Service solar panels provided covered parking for 144 parking spaces while providing cost savings to SVdP Phoenix. The project was completed on June 1, 2019.

We are so grateful for its generosity to our mission and to the volunteers and donors who work with us to serve others."

As part of the APS Solar Communities Program, which partners with established nonprofits to provide solar-generating parking panels across Arizona, the project at SVdP Phoenix was the inaugural construction and installation project in the program. "This is a blessing and tremendous gift to our organization and to those we serve in so many ways," said Zabilski. The project was coordinated by SVdP Phoenix senior advisor Steve Gervais, who submitted the application to APS and managed the project, which began construction in February 2019 and was completed in June 2019. Gervais said:

> *It was an honor for St. Vincent de Paul to be selected as the first site under the APS Solar Communities Program for Non-Profits in Arizona. By any standard, this was no small project. It was a pleasure to work with our partners at APS and their contractor Harmon Electric. They did a great job completing the project on schedule with no disruption to operations at St. Vincent de Paul. The panels were fully installed, wired to "the grid" and began generating solar energy by the middle of June 2019, right on schedule.*

While there is no doubt that generosity, hard work, care for one's neighbor and community spirit all power the work of the world's largest council of St. Vincent de Paul, there can also be no doubt that plenty of power comes from the APS solar panels in its parking lot.

SVdP Phoenix is a face-to-face responder to poverty. It cooperates with fellow charitable organizations, but it only joins others if it has a direct contact with the assistance provided. A good example of this is its partnership with the Phoenix Human Services Campus (HSC). The society joined this consortium of charitable services because it provides an efficient way to serve people without housing and because the society can directly provide daily meals within the campus environment. The society considers its face-to-face response a key part of its services.

The HSC recently underwent a change of structure. Most of the land of the homeless campus was owned by Maricopa County. In 2017, the Maricopa County board of directors voted unanimously to approve the transfer of the land from the county to the new campus organization. The new structure also created a new campus board of directors with enhanced authority over the running of the campus. Previously, the old board consisted of just a few executives from the nonprofit partners; now, the board is composed of seventeen members, with two board seats allocated to SVdP Phoenix. In 2020, the board president is Jonathan Koppell, PhD; the SVdP Phoenix positions are filled by past SVdP Phoenix board president Joe Riley and chief financial officer Marcus Anderson.

Chapter 8 discussed the crisis of the asylum-seeking families and how SVdP Phoenix responded to that emergency. SVdP Phoenix not only responded directly to the crisis but joined with other groups to find a more sustainable solution, including partnering with the international rescue committee to set up a collaborative, long-term welcome center for asylum-seeking families. The society's main role in the development of this project was to provide a majority of the meals and travel food needed for the new facility. The welcome center accepted its first group of families on July 27, 2019. As of September 2019, all was working as planned, and a transition was made to a much-improved outreach. A converted grade school, formerly known as the Ann Ott School located near downtown Phoenix, was selected as the site for the welcome center. The new welcome center is perfectly located near SVdP Phoenix's Dan O'Meara Center as well as the Greyhound station and airport. It is dedicated to its intended effort twenty-four hours a day; thus, there is no moving of cots and tables, and there is no set-up and take-down to accommodate other programs in the same space. It is a wonderful accomplishment for the community.

With as many organizations that volunteer with SVdP Phoenix, there are many who wish to partner with the society to expand or enhance its existing programs. A long list of organizations through established partnerships provide financial and service assistance. But the society's partnership with Arizona State University (ASU) provides special benefits, both in the types of service the society provides and in the fact that it is engaging young students in helping those who are less fortunate. These students are the community of the future and will provide a future legacy for SVdP Phoenix.

For as long as anyone can remember, there have been collaborative touchpoints between Arizona State University and SVdP Phoenix. A more formal partnership began in the late 1980s, when Dr. Phillip Mizzi, an associate professor of economics in the ASU W.P. Carey School of Business, moved to Arizona and started volunteering with SVdP Phoenix. His connection with the society rapidly developed to include staff, students and other faculty members who joined him in service and research opportunities. Mizzi joined the SVdP Phoenix board of directors in 2008 and served in this role for several years. During a conversation in 2016, St. Vincent de Paul leadership and ASU president Michael Crow discussed the many ways in which ASU and SVdP Phoenix could partner together, recognizing that the scope and depth of possible partnerships had significantly increased. They also determined that there were opportunities for partnerships that could benefit both agencies. Strengthening the case for a formalized partnership were the many ASU alumni who were serving as members of the Vinnies, SVdP Phoenix's professional advisory board. Members of this group were already forging collaborations with ASU, tapping into faculty research expertise, students' eagerness for socially embedded academic projects, and the institutions' joint interests in a strong downtown Phoenix. The Vinnies informally coordinated many of these touchpoints and added to an already compelling narrative cocreating a stronger, more resilient Arizona.

In the spring of 2016, the ASU Educational Outreach Student Services (EOSS) unit held a gathering of ASU units, including academic and student support, that had partnered with SVdP Phoenix. During that discussion, the ASU partners that represented all four ASU campuses were asked to describe the length and breadth of their SVdP Phoenix partnership. The society recommended setting up fifty-nine touchpoints between ASU and SVdP Phoenix, including 1,072 students doing service, four community-informed research projects, eighteen group service projects, twenty-four internships, eleven examples of knowledge exchange or resource sharing and ten connections with faculty. This inventory reflected the strength of the partnership and diversity in activities which led to the formalization of the partnership in 2017.

In addition to the history of interwoven touchpoints, both organizations share similar values and have innovative organizational footprints in their respective fields. The value of inclusiveness is foundational for both SVdP Phoenix and ASU. SVdP Phoenix emphasizes the importance of serving those who have no alternative for help, and ASU measures its success not by whom it excludes but by whom it includes. There are also groups and businesses that support both organizations.

The partnership was formalized through a memorandum of understanding in July 2017; it set priorities and initiated a jointly funded staff position, which is currently held by Erica Hodges, the ASU and SVdP Phoenix program manager. Multiple ASU units and SVdP Phoenix departments are now engaging to increase connectivity between academic disciplines, student support services and community needs. There are 491 mutually beneficial touchpoints, including 35 faculty connections, 71 groups that have engaged in service, 87 student internships and 2,554 students who served as volunteers, which resulted in 16,120 hours of service.

At the start of the formal partnership in the fall of 2017, ten broad priorities had been identified, including three research focus areas. They included:

- Research initiatives (health and well-being, homelessness reunification and program evaluation).
- Urban farm innovation.
- Program evaluation and enhancement of data collection.
- Partnership inventory.
- Student service.
- Student experiential opportunities.
- College access and youth development.
- Enhancing retail operations.
- Staff professional development.
- Cultivation of national community service organizations on behalf of ASU and St. Vincent de Paul.

These priorities were identified through discussions with SVdP Phoenix departments, leadership and through the ASU and Society Partnership Inventory.

As the partnership has evolved, the priority areas have been condensed to:

- Models of partnership (highlight the ways in which the partnership has made progress).
- Building partnership capacity.
- Volunteerism and experiential learning.
- Innovative solutions to homelessness prevention.

The components of research, evaluation, mutual staff development, innovation and impact cut across all of these areas. The following highlights are examples of strong and reciprocal partnership activities and outcomes:

USE-INSPIRED RESEARCH: Dr. Gabriel Shaibi PhD, research faculty for the ASU college of nursing and healthcare innovation and the SVdP Virginia G. Piper Medical Clinic family wellness program have partnered for over ten years to create health promotion and diabetes prevention programs for high-risk and vulnerable Latino youth and families. Their partnership is featured in the 2018 ASU *Social Embeddedness* magazine. Dr. Shaibi and the family wellness program won the ASU president's *Social Embeddedness* Award.

BUILDING PARTNERSHIP CAPACITY: The W.P. Carey School of Business supply chain management department has been working with SVdP Phoenix since the late 1990s. Dr. Phil Mizzi, an associate professor of economics, and Dr. Mohan Gopalakrishnan, a professor and chair of supply chain management, prepared an analysis of the SVdP food reclamation process, which resulted in a publication, several grants and more efficient processes in the SVdP Phoenix food warehouse. W.P. Carey faculty continue to support the partnership with SVdP Phoenix through research and applied graduate projects. Dr. Mayhar Eftekhar, an assistant professor, is researching the evolution of a volunteer's monetary giving. Gregory Collins, a lecturer, supported four MBA students who consulted with Jen Morgan, the SVdP Phoenix resource center manager, in the creation of a tool and process to more accurately track incoming donations at the society's resource center. The students spent approximately seventy-eight hours on this project for a total cost of $22,160, based on a contract rate of $80 per hour.

URBAN FARMS: In 2016, SVdP Phoenix received $1 million from the Rob and Melani Walton Foundation to create a two-acre urban farm in partnership with ASU's Walton Sustainability Solutions Initiatives (WSSI). The SVdP Phoenix and ASU WSSI partnership created appropriate methods and targets to increase the social, environmental and economic impact of SVdP Phoenix's Rob and Melani Walton Urban Farm, which opened in January 2018.

Currently, the WSSI is providing technical assistance to ASU sustainability student Maddie Mercer, who is creating a guide on social impact through urban farming based on her work at the urban farm. Mercer recently received an ASU Changemaker Woodside Community Action Grant of $700 to extend the SVdP Phoenix Urban Farming Together program to three local title 1 schools. Her proposal will also receive $3,000 as a result of the SVdP Phoenix partnership with United Way.

The ASU Engineering Projects in Community Service (EPICS) high school program at Metro Tech High School has also completed a water reclamation project, contributing over $3,000 in building supplies. The funnel system that was designed by students will reclaim rainwater and air-conditioning runoff that gathers on the roof of an SVdP Phoenix building. SVdP Phoenix contributed an additional $500 for building supplies and staff to construct the catch system.

ASYLUM SEEKERS: In 2019, SVdP Phoenix partnered with the International Rescue Committee (IRC) and Phoenix Restoration Project (PRP) to support families going through the legal process of seeking asylum. SVdP Phoenix extended hospitality services six days a week to individuals and families who were in a state of transition, on their way to being reunited with family. Three new staff members facilitated the program; two were ASU alumni. This coalition submitted a concept summary for the creation of a community shelter facility to the Arizona Grantmakers Forum, which is based on some of the information from the SVdP Asylum Relief Center. The ASU EOSS unit has been supported by a coordinated effort to connect the coalition that supports asylum seekers with ASU resources.

EDUCATION: In December 2017, ASU, the Maricopa Community College District (MCCD) and SVdP Phoenix partnered on a pilot program to increase Latino student access and educational attainment. Based on feedback from the families involved with the pilot program, biweekly parent and youth programming focused on accessing higher education has continued with the support of ASU's Access program, including SPARKS, the American Dream Academy and First Star Academy, among others. Additionally, fourteen of the twenty-eight SVdP Phoenix One at a Time (OAAT) scholars attend ASU; four of these ASU students graduated in 2019. Monthly OAAT scholar and mentor workshops and support for scholars continue. Jessie Helmes, the internship support coordinator for the ASU College of Health Solutions and a master in higher education student, is conducting research on the mentor relationship component of SVdP Phoenix's OAAT program.

HOMELESSNESS PREVENTION AND TRANSFORM SOCIETY: In the fall of 2018, ASU, SVdP Phoenix and Miracle Messages (a supported project of the Netroots Foundation) partnered on an initiative designed to reunite people experiencing homelessness with their families and friends. Jessica Berg, the SVdP Phoenix chief program officer, collaborated with Dr. Sandy Price, a lecturer in the ASU School of Community Resources and Development, on Dr. Price's fall 2018 course on piloting this homeless family reunification program. Students interviewed and recorded stories and messages from guests to their loved ones. The students then took on the role of "digital detectives" to deliver the Miracle Messages by using social media and online tools. They reached families as far away as Kansas City and Missouri and as local as Scottsdale, reuniting six of the twenty-five guests who were interviewed.

11

UNENDING MISSION OF MERCY

The Society of St. Vincent de Paul began in 1833 in Paris, France, and came to the United States in 1845. It arrived in Phoenix, Arizona, in 1946. The general message articulated by the founder of St. Vincent de Paul, Blessed Frederic Ozanam, was that the society must make itself available to directly help those in need of assistance. As he did, the society's members should see the face of Christ in the poor. Frederic's dreams of embracing the whole world in a network of charity became a reality. Today, ordinary men and women, some eight hundred thousand strong, by the grace of God, do extraordinary things for the poor, regardless of race, creed, color or status.

SVdP Phoenix was started by a group of men who wanted to respond to the needs of people who were living in poverty. SVdP Phoenix began slowly and struggled to establish itself. As it began to grow and expand its services, the number of people needing assistance also continued to grow. Spirituality has always been important to the society's members, but organization and common sense have also played an important part in the society's success. The society's general philosophy ("No work of charity is foreign to the society") is a major factor in what has allowed it to provide assistance wherever it is needed.

Just as human hopes, dreams and values know no geographical boundaries, neither do the needs experienced by the poor. Whether it be Argentina or Australia—India or Italy—Mexico or Myanmar—Singapore or Spain—Uganda or Ukraine, the Vincentian family is there to help. Let's add to that Avondale or Ash Fork—Cave Creek or Cottonwood—Flagstaff or Fountain Hills—Glendale or Gila Bend—Prescott or Peoria—Sedona or Surprise—Tempe or Tuba City—Kingman or Lake Havasu—or anywhere in the city of Phoenix. Vincentians consider it a privilege to be part of such a worthy endeavor that spreads God's boundless, unconditional love so far and wide and touches so many lives.

Through structured programs, the society is able to provide direct assistance with food, medical, dental, financial and housing needs to individuals and families who are experiencing poverty and challenges associated with poverty. It has responded to emergency crises that have temporarily erupted throughout the state, crises that have included aiding the victims of the Arizona Rodeo Chedisky fire and helping the refugees entering Arizona from south of the border in Mexico. The society's help comes both from its developed programs and its unique ability to go where there is an immediate need. The ministry of SVdP's parish-based conferences is the bridge that connects the Gospel to the needs of God's people. It is at this grass-roots level that the great majority of Vincentians encounter poverty firsthand and respond with love, hope and help, one person at a time.

Since the society's founding, the central and most basic activity of its conferences has been visiting the needy in their homes. It is there, in the family setting, that Vincentians listen attentively, without judging, offer advice humbly and assist in a respectful way that preserves the dignity of the persons they serve. Making God present to the poor through a loving, reassuring presence and restoring hope to those who have none is a life-changing act of love. When someone who has lost hope discovers there are people who truly care, then something magical—even miraculous—can happen.

The quiet work of the society's conferences is often unseen, yet its scope and substance are significant. In 2019, the Vincentians of SVdP Phoenix made nearly 45,000 home visits, delivered almost 181,000 food boxes and gave more than $4.6 million in direct aid to those in need. Add to that the members' visits to hospitals, nursing homes, assisted-living facilities and prisons. In all, conference members and volunteers devoted more than 502,000 hours to their labors of love. This assistance combines with the activities at the society's five dining rooms, seventeen thrift stores, medical and dental clinic, Food Reclamation Center, Ozanam Manor, Transient Aid Center, Ministry to the Homeless and urban farms to form the protective safety net that St. Vincent de Paul provides to its neighbors in need.

Frederic Ozanam believed that "Christianity is not about ideas but about deeds inspired by love." The society is greatly blessed by the goodness and generosity of countless caring people whose love for the less fortunate of

God's children enables its Vincentians to joyfully perform such deeds on a daily basis.

An essential aspect of the society's place in its communities is the belief its benefactors have in it; they make it possible for SVdP Phoenix to feed, clothe, house and heal so many people. The society considers that belief to be a sacred trust, one it strives to honor fully every day.

SVdP is committed to fostering a community in which everyone looks out for each other, everyone has faith in each other, as members of one family. The society will always do its best to help alleviate suffering, even while the growing population of Arizona has resulted in an escalating need for its services. It is only limited by the resources available. SVdP Phoenix is deeply grateful for the community's support, which has allowed it to be the most successful SVdP in the world. St. Teresa of Calcutta said to give the poor "not only your care but also your heart." The Vincentians of SVdP Phoenix, together with the society's volunteers, employees and donors, have demonstrated through the past seventy-four years that they care deeply and give their hearts generously. Their exceptional love of their neighbors reflects the legacy of those men in 1946 who were called to serve their suffering brothers and sisters. The society's founder would no doubt wholeheartedly agree. Jesus Christ once said, "The poor will always be with you," but how we respond to poverty may be the primary factor our final judgment will depend on.